Lies
I Told Myself,
& Other Truths

Lies
I Told Myself,
& Other Truths

*HOW TO SQUASH THE MENTAL
MONSTERS AND LIVE YOUR DREAMS*

NIKKI SOULSBY

For information about special discounts for bulk purchases, please contact Nikki Soulsby at info@nikkisoulsby.com

Edited by Clarify Editing & The Write Edit

ISBN 978-1-7371358-0-7 (paperback)
ISBN 978-1-7371358-1-4 (eBook)

For Greg, who believed I could.
I love you.

Table of Contents

Introduction

"Who do you think you are?" Michael Scott[1] is not giving you an exit interview; this is a real question.

Who *do* you think you are?

You answer is directly related to my next question: What do you deserve?

What you think about yourself determines what you believe you are worth. Like it or not, what you believe you're worth is what you get, because it's what you're willing to accept. It's like that scene in *Pretty Woman*[2] where Julia Roberts is shopping on Rodeo Drive and gets run off by nasty, judgy saleswomen. She had money to spend and she knew it, but she let those women kick her out because she didn't feel worthy of having nice things. After a little coaching from Richard Gere on what kind of service she should expect, Roberts has no trouble holding her ground and demanding her value for the rest of the film.

Roberts starts out in the gutter because she allowed herself and other people to put her there. She is the same person at the end of the movie as she was at the start, with a modification. She changed what she thought about herself. When she first entered the Beverly Wilshire Hotel, she was visibly uncomfortable. By the end of the movie, she had plans to move, finish her high school diploma, and get a day job. All because she figured out she was worth more. This, my sweet friend, is true for all of us.

"It's not who you are that holds you back, it is who you think you're not," says author and speaker Denis Waitley.[3]

The quality of your life hinges on what you're willing to accept, and that comes from what you believe about yourself, the world, and other people. You have to get your mind right to get your life right.

Your brain is the most powerful tool in your arsenal. You can use it either for good or for evil. My brain, if allowed, will turn into a toddler and wreak havoc everywhere. It will find the absolute worst times to remind me of unhelpful things, it will get distracted when I need to focus, and it will tell me to accept less than I deserve, because who the hell do I think I am anyway? The good news is that my thoughts are in my control. If I can control my thoughts, I can control my actions. If I can control my actions, I can control my life. I don't know about you, but I want more out of life, which means I have to ask more of myself.

The number one thing that held me back from getting the good life was what I thought. The really awful part is that a lot of those thoughts weren't even true. I was lying to myself, and it almost cost me everything. At my low point, I was depressed, in debt, miserable, working at a soul-sucking job, hoping I could pay my bills, certain I didn't deserve love, frustrated that bad things always happened to me, and toying with the idea of not waking up tomorrow. I was desperate for my life to improve.

Motivational speaker, author, and business tycoon, Tony Robbins says your life changes for one of two reasons: inspiration or desperation.[4] I was definitely the second. I didn't want things in my life to get better, I *needed* them to get better. And they did get better. Not overnight, but over time my life changed dramatically. I went from being unemployed to being a rising star at a Fortune 50 company. I went from being a victim of sexual abuse to having a healthy marriage with a doting husband. I went from being tens of thousands of dollars in debt to being debt free and nearly tripling my income. I went from suicidal to joyful and thriving. All because I changed my thoughts.

It started when my life fell apart, but crystallized for me in grad school. One homework assignment showed me that I had been living a lie for over a decade. This lie was stunting my present and future. Once I identified the lie, I was able to replace it with truth. I took that opportunity to examine all of my beliefs and keep only what was helpful and true. It's like that biblical verse in Philippians 4:8: "Whatever is true, whatever is noble, whatever is right, whatever is pure, whatever is lovely, whatever is admirable— if anything is excellent or praiseworthy—think about such things."

I jumped on the self-help bandwagon in 2008. While my roommates were seeing the latest movies, listening to Lady Gaga, and going to frat parties, I was reading Dale Carnegie, listening to motivational speakers, and attending business conferences. My actions didn't help my popularity, but they did teach me valuable success principles. However, *knowing* success principles and *living* success principles are different things. Turns out, if you keep your self-limiting beliefs, you keep your circumstances, no matter how many success principles you can recite. You can't outwork negative thought patterns. It's like trying to run off every calorie you ate today. You will run out of energy or hurt yourself before you zero out. When you allow your brain to get stuck in negative or unhelpful thought patterns, you cripple your success before you even get off the starting line.

I know you have dreams. Even if you can't clearly articulate those dreams at this moment, I know they exist. Maybe your dream is some peace (and quiet), financial stability, ownership of your time, meaningful work, respect, love. Maybe you just want a decent night's sleep. All dreams are valid here. The thing about dreams is they are meant to be more than just fantasy. They are meant to be lived. There is no point in torturing yourself with "impossible" dreams because you're chained by your brain.

If you don't read another word of this book I want you to know three things:

1. You can have the life you dream about. You deserve it, you're worth it, you can do it.
2. If it's not working, do something about it or change your attitude.
3. You're not alone.

The rest of the book is going to cover lies I told myself, how I squashed those lies, and how you can squash them too. I realize that my mental monsters may not be the same as yours, but I believe you'll find something relatable and encouraging in my stories.

Do I have this nailed? No way! There are times when I slip up and fall right back into my old thought patterns. Now that I'm aware they exist, I can more easily identify them, squash them, and replace them with truth that removes limits from my potential.

By the end of this book, you will be able to tackle the things holding you back from the life you deserve. I believe in you. I believe in your dreams, your hopes, and your desires. I believe that you are capable of more. Author A.A. Milne was right in saying, "You are braver than you believe, stronger than you seem, and smarter than you think."[5] Friend, you can move mountains. So let's start living those better lives today. Let's slay those mental monsters and make your dreams come true.

I Am a Mean Person

MY mom is full of advice. As a good daughter, I listen to most of it and then do whatever I want. Every once in a while, she comes up with something really good:

1. It's just as easy to fall in love with a rich man as it is a poor man.
2. Don't drink. But when you do, don't have more than two.
3. Don't be mean, Nikki, it's not nice.

The third one is my favorite. For a long time, this was just a funny thing my mom said. She also says "to the moon, Alice"[6] when I'm in big trouble. So we can't really take her literally. When she would say "Don't be mean, it's not nice," it was usually because I was being a sassy little shit. Then something happened that made me believe that there was more than humor behind my mom's words.

I went to undergrad at a tiny women's college in central Virginia. This statement is usually met with "I could never …" coupled with pearl clutching. Listen, going to a women's college is just like going to a coed college, only you don't have to care about looking nice for class. Also, there is no fighting for gender equality in a classroom. Women's opinions are heard because there's no one there to talk louder. You are encouraged to break norms, be a leader, and think differently. All of this sounds awesome, and it is, but it's still a school full of girls, complete with the drama and cliques.

Oh, how I wanted to be popular! I wanted to be one of the shiny, beautiful people who dripped with glamour and friends and awesomeness. There was one shiny person who was especially perplexing. She was not a blonde glamazon. She didn't come from money. She didn't even wear the right clothes. But she was magnetizing. She has that *je ne sais quoi*, something you can't quite put your finger on that sucks you in.

The first time I saw her, she was sauntering across the lower quad, *Teenage Mutant Ninja Turtles* T-shirt on, rainbow-studded belt, and tattoos. She walked like she knew who she was and where she was going. I wanted that. I wanted to be that or be around that, and I knew I had to get to know her.

When the entire student population is seven hundred, getting to know someone isn't challenging. Except this time. For months I'd catch glimpses of the unicorn, but always in passing and always surrounded by friends. I suppose I could have hollered at her and waved her down, but the thing about unicorns is they are easily spooked. And one should not wave down strangers with Muppet arms and shouting unless one has a good reason. Anyway, my patience eventually paid off.

One of my five campus jobs was that of head teaching assistant for the public speaking course. The unicorn happened to be in this class, and I happened to be the one assigning mentors (*creepy eyebrow waggle*). With 100 percent self-interest, I selected myself to be her mentor. This meant I met with her outside of class to provide feedback on topics or coach her through practice sessions. She *had* to talk to me. If all went according to plan we would maybe, one day, be friends.

After our second meeting, she looked me dead in the face and said, "You're not as bad as I thought you'd be."

What?! My eyes bugged slightly before I responded with, "What do you mean?"

"I don't know. You always seemed like such a bitch."

I inhaled deeply and let this marinate. *Me? A bitch?* She went on to explain that my demeanor was intimidating and aloof. I immediately called up a mental picture of how I must look to other people. Since I was taking more than a full course load *and* had five part-time jobs, I was always rushing to and from places. In the few minutes between obligations, I'd make mental lists of to do's and obligations. However, other people didn't know what I was thinking, and I could imagine I had a nasty case of resting bitch face (RBF). Not good. In addition to an off-putting countenance, I was shy, which can easily be interpreted as rude. Damn, maybe I was a jerk.

During the next couple of years, I made desperate attempts to curtail my bitchiness. I smiled more and went out of my way to be friendly and helpful. But no matter how much I did for anyone, it still felt like I was on the outside looking in. I assumed that people didn't want to be friends with someone mean, and so my social circle stayed small.

My fear was realized two years later over coffee. I had joined a network marketing business and had done enough work to get recognized by one of the leaders of the organization. My heart sang. I got to have coffee with someone tremendously successful, and she was going to teach me the secrets of building a successful business and living an exceptional life. During our chat it came up that I had offended someone else on the team. I gave this other person tough love that they weren't ready for, and they went bawling to the people in charge. What started as a pleasant coffee turned quickly into a (professional) chewing out. The leader acknowledged that nothing I said was incorrect or inappropriate. The person was simply not ready for the truth, and I overstepped by giving it to them. During this coaching moment, the leader stated bluntly that I was a mean person and people didn't like me.

I waited for the JK, JK, but it didn't come. She was completely serious. My first reaction was denial. If I was being mean on purpose, you would *know* I was being mean. I knew I hadn't said anything cruel or disheartening. In fact, my purpose in telling the truth had been to help the other person. This was ridiculous. I steamed for the rest of the coffee and left in a grump.

After the shock wore off, I reassessed the situation. This was a leader I deeply respected. She had the life I wanted, and it was in my best interest to do what she said. She wouldn't tell me something that would hurt me. My meanness must be a blind spot. I couldn't see it in myself, but everyone else noticed. She must have told me this to help me change and become the successful person I dreamed of being. I accepted her judgment as truth in 2009.

The thought of who I really was horrified me. I did not want to be known as the asshole of our group. Does anyone? I proceeded to read every self-help book I could find on interpersonal skills, including *How to Win Friends and Influence People* (seven times). I wrote affirmations to say to myself everyday:

- I am vanilla and palatable.
- I am kind.
- I make friends easily.

I worked on myself for years. It didn't help, though. Every time (or maybe every other time) I went for a coaching session with that woman, she brought up how mean I was and how people didn't like me. The last time we spoke, nearly a decade after our first conversation, she told me I would never be successful because I was just a mean person. I was gutted, but only a little. I had long ago accepted that I was just a rotten individual.

The lie: **I am a mean person.**

* * *

How I squashed the lie:

I started seeing a therapist after the network marketing company and I parted ways. The first thing out of his mouth when I told him my story was, "How long were you emotionally abused by this woman?" I counted back and it had been about ten years. I never thought of it as emotional abuse, but who was I to argue with a professional? It took a couple years of cognitive behavioral therapy to get to a point where my depression wasn't crushing. Despite the improvement in my general mental health, I didn't stop believing that I was mean and that no one liked me.

Three years later, while getting my MBA from Duke, I took a class on brand management. During the personal branding session, we did an exercise to determine how other people perceived our brand. I surveyed thirty people. These were my findings:

- I am ambitious, intelligent, kind.
- I am not patient, nurturing, or seasoned.

I was **kind**. In my book, kind is better than nice. These people who worked with me, lived with me, and knew me intimately believed that I was double-plus good. They could have picked any word to describe me, and they picked that one. Y'all, I'm not a crier, but I shed tears over this revelation. I had spent a decade believing that I was an asshole and that my friends were my friends mostly out of fear and intimidation. I had no idea my friends were genuine and not a single one of them thought I was mean. I tried to challenge some of these people on their opinion. I tried to *prove* my meanness to them. I thought maybe they were bullshitting me to help my grade. They all thought I was fishing for compliments.

I knew that other people lied to themselves all the time. I didn't realize I did too. I am practical and self-aware. I wouldn't believe lies about myself. But I couldn't argue with facts. There it was in dozens of anonymous survey results provided by people who know me best. I was not mean.

* * *

How you can squash it too:

What negative things have you internalized as truths for yourself? Are you mean? Are you lazy? Are you obnoxious? Are you ugly? Are you underqualified? Are you unworthy?

Sometimes the answer is obvious, and other times it takes a little help to figure this out. I recommend two things to help you uncover your untruths. First, you must get a picture of who you are according to you. Think bigger than what roles you play, like mother, employee, or friend. Think about what makes you, you. What are your traits and quirks? What are your values? You can search "values list" and look at the image results for ideas about what values are.

Once you've got a good idea of how you see yourself, I suggest doing your own personal branding exercise. You need to ask at least ten people representing at least two areas of your life (home and work) for their opinions. You want to know two things:

1.   What are three words that describe me?
2.   What are three positive things I am not?

I recommend creating an anonymous survey in order to get the most honest answers and organize them easily. Ensure your survey participants that you will not react to their answers. This is easier to do when you don't know who said what. But be prepared for constructive criticism. If you are not currently aware of any shortcomings, this might not be a pleasant exercise.

When all of the results are in, you can analyze your brand. Find the trends. If one person said you're a hot mess, you can throw out that opinion. They must have been having a bad day. If eight people said you're a hot mess, well, maybe that's something you want to work on. Look for the things that come up over and over again. Those offer the best indication of how you are presenting to the world. Do these trends line up with how you see yourself?

"Evidence suggests that people are actually more keen to receive constructive (critical) rather than positive feedback. A study by *Harvard Business Review* found that 57 percent of people would prefer constructive feedback to positive praise or recognition."[7] This means that if you're like most people, you will have a harder time accepting the good things about yourself than the bad things about yourself. The thing we are looking for here is self-limiting beliefs. Self-limiting beliefs are things you believe about yourself, other people, or the world that are holding you back.

Harvard Professor Dr. John Sharp advises three steps to conquering self-limiting beliefs in his TEDx Talk "Change Your Story, Transform Your Life."[8]

1.   Be compassionate.

Being hard on yourself is not going to help here. Yes, there are probably some things you've bought into that are keeping you from achieving your goals. Welcome to the club. Everyone believes dumb stuff from time to time.

For more than twenty years, I believed ostriches put their heads in the sand when they were afraid. Then a friend told me this was a myth; if ostriches really did bury their heads in the sand, they would suffocate. When I sat back and thought about it, the whole notion of hiding in the sand seemed kind of ridiculous. But it didn't seem ridiculous until someone taught me better.

When you're identifying self-limiting beliefs, you don't need to add condemnation to the process. Unlearning stuff is hard, even if it's beneficial. Be as gracious and forgiving to yourself as you would a friend. I bet that if your friend, who has had low self-esteem the entire time you've known her, figured out that she was even half as awesome as she is, you would be on top of the table popping a bottle of prosecco. You would not say *God, Brenda, get over yourself.*

2.   Detach from false truth.

To paraphrase the Buddha, *Let that shit go.* Once you identify the lies, it's time to squash them. I loathe cockroaches. They are gross, ugly, and terrifying. They are not allowed in my house. Period. When one crawls in here, I don't ask it to pull up a chair and have a drink. No, I grab the Raid and spray until it stops moving. Then I get the vacuum and suck it into oblivion. For you brave souls who can step on them and not gag, please still be my friend. The point is, when something isn't welcome in your house, you kill it and take it far away. You don't keep it around to remind you of worse times. The same thing applies to your brain. You are the *maître d'* at Chez [your name]. You get to decide what thoughts are permitted a seat at the table. Choose wisely.

3. Install a new narrative.

Your brain and your stomach have more in common than you think. One, they are always working. Two, when they run out of fuel they are demanding. If you keep good food in your stomach, it won't yell at you, send you snooping in the pantry for your hidden chocolate stash, or make you hangry. If you leave it on empty for too long, all bets are off. You could go face first into some Taco Bell and regret it about twenty minutes later. Then you're sore, still hungry, and looking for anything to make you feel better. Mmm, celery, right?

When you take away a thought your brain is used to having, it leaves a hole. The easiest thing to do is replace the hole with the thing you removed. However, you chose to get rid of that thought in the first place—you don't want to put it back. So you need to have a new thought primed and ready to go every time the old thought tries to sneak in. I use affirmations to help me with this. When my lie about being mean creeps in, I swap it out for: *I have a sweet spirit. People like me. I am generous and kind.*

At first this kind of self-talk is weird. It feels wrong because you're trying to put a different-shaped thought into the hole left by the lie. That's okay. Your brain will adjust. Eventually you'll believe the truth first. And the truth does set you free.

When you love and accept every part of yourself, life gets so much simpler. You don't have to waste energy on fighting invisible monsters. There are plenty of problems out there that require your best. Don't waste any of your time, energy, or talent on false accusations.

P.S. The unicorn from undergrad and I did become friends after that public speaking class. She is one of the three people from college I talk to regularly twelve years later. The good news is that she only thinks I'm a bitch now when I'm acting like one. Which is totally fair.

CHAPTER 2

I Don't Deserve It

IN 2017 I got put in my place.

I had been working for a financial advising firm for about two years and I was crushing it. I was the backbone of my department and would often joke that they would have to hire two people to replace me if I ever left. Our company decided to transition to a new software system. This meant an upgrade in features, but it also meant months of a doubled workload. My supervisor didn't think I could handle the extra work in addition to my normal responsibilities (oh, ye of little faith) and hired someone to help.

The new girl and I became fast friends. We had a morning ritual of getting coffee together in the break room and also did the occasional lunch. I was having a blast. I got to slay work all day and gossip to my office bestie when I had some downtime. At one of our lunches, my friend casually mentioned how much the company was paying her. It was more than me. Quite a bit more than me. I like this girl a lot, but there was nothing in her background to warrant a better salary. I felt betrayed, frustrated, and angry, but I asked her how she got that number. She said she used an online calculator to figure out what the industry standards were for this position and then asked for that when they hired her.

Obviously I immediately calculated what my position was worth. (Glassdoor.com and LinkedIn.com both have salary estimators that do a good job of showing you industry trends based on location, title, industry, experience, and education.) Given my experience, education, and background, I should have been making $15,000 more annually.

I'm not brazen. I knew I couldn't just march into my boss's office and demand more money. So I started keeping a list of all the extra projects I worked on and all the stats around my normal work. In about a month, I had enough material to put together a presentation on the value I was bringing to the company and how aligning my salary with the industry standard was an equitable decision for them. Sounds great, right?

It didn't exactly go over like I planned. My boss was furious with the request. She told me I should be grateful to be employed at all because my skills were not as impressive as I thought. Also, I would not be getting a raise of any kind or a bonus. I didn't deserve it.

Three months later, during my performance evaluation, I got exceptional marks for all of my work, and also a "does not meet expectations" general comment. She made sure to include both (tiny) mistakes I'd made that year, for supporting evidence as to why I was a liability for the company. I went from disappointed to heartbroken. I had done my best at this job and they thought I was trash.

I took the next six months and tried to support other departments and find new opportunities. People were happy to hand off projects for me to finish, but they didn't want to hire me as a part of their team. The chief HR officer pulled me into his office one day and told me to stop. Stop trying to move out of my department and stop applying for open positions. I was not going to be considered. In fact, they felt like they'd made a mistake by hiring me because I was both creative and analytical. I didn't fit into one box or the other. So they didn't know what to do with me.

I knew then that this company was not a place where I could build a career and doubled my effort in looking for opportunities at other companies. When asked what I expected for my salary, I told them to match the number I was already making. I didn't apply to a single job that would have stretched me professionally. All of my applications were for positions I'd already held; some were even steps backward! My boss's valuation rang loudly in my ears.

The lie: I don't deserve it.

***

How I squashed the lie:

Value is subjective. Maurizio Cattelan duct taped a banana to a wall and called it art. This installation sold for $120,000.[9] It also created quite the stir both inside and outside of the art community.[10] Cattelan named the price, but it actually acquired its value when it sold. It sold for three times that price (or higher)!

There are two ways to look at the price of art: intrinsic value and assigned value. Intrinsic value is what a thing is worth in and of itself. A banana and a piece of tape aren't worth much. By my calculation, they might be worth twenty cents.[11] However, when someone takes these items and puts them together in a social critique of the art world, they take on a new value. They are assigned a value based on the context. Experts may argue about what the piece is worth, but ultimately, what it sells for is a representation of the assigned value.

When I worked for that company, I allowed them to assign my value to me. They decided my salary, my projects, and my potential for advancement. All companies do this. Your salary is calculated based on your contribution to the company in that role and comparable salaries in the industry. You are not paid for your intrinsic value, which includes your potential. You are paid what the position is worth. There is nothing wrong with accepting a reasonable wage for your work. The problem comes when you allow other people's assigned value to overwrite the intrinsic value you possess.

When I sat down and thought about it, I realized I was being undervalued. The boss who told me I was no good got a promotion after taking credit for my work. The company clearly valued the contribution I made, but they incorrectly assigned the credit to her. If my work wasn't good, why did she take credit for it? If I didn't deserve more money, why did she get a raise? It didn't add up.

Eventually one of my interviews paid off. I was offered a position at another company making $17,000 more. Muahahaha! Not only did this company give me more money, but they also empowered me to be my best. In my first eighteen months, I got promoted twice, which increased my pay, responsibilities, and visibility at the company. Part of these results came from working in an environment that supported growth, innovation, and initiative. The bigger part of the results came from understanding that my job title and salary had nothing to do with what I was worth or what I could become.

My growth at the company sounds sexy when I leave out the bad parts. Yes, I found ways to advance, but they weren't always the most obvious moves. I had several supervisors tell me I wasn't qualified for promotions, deserving of more money, or worthy of being invited to meetings with important people. Get some new material, people! That line is tired.

Since I'd already conquered this lie, I knew how to respond. I refused to accept this judgment and kept bringing my best to work. People didn't get to decide when I was done; I did. I ended up with three simultaneous job offers (two internal and one from a competitor) and leveraged the power of multiple offers to negotiate more meaningful work, a better title, and more money. It was a good move.

Am I getting paid what I'm worth? Not even close, but I'm making almost triple what I was getting paid at that financial advising firm.

***

How you can squash it too:

Valuation is complicated, because it relies heavily on context and preferences. I'm an econ geek and get super excited when we start talking about utility, I mean, valuation. When you put a value on something you try to be objective, but that's simply not possible. There is no objectivity about what something is worth.

There are three things I want you to keep in mind when assigning value to yourself.

1. Don't take things for granted.

There's an economic principle called the law of diminishing returns that says the more you have of something the less valuable it is (context). The most common example given for this is the water vs. diamonds paradox. Your next glass of tap water is going to cost you a negligible amount of money. You won't even think twice before turning on the tap to brush your teeth. However, you'll probably put quite a bit of thought into the next diamond purchase you make. Water is essential to life and diamonds are not. So why is water so inexpensive? It took economists hundreds of years to come up with a good answer.

Diamonds are scarce, meaning they aren't piling up in the street. Water, in abundant times, is almost free because there is a lot of it. If you're in the middle of a drought, though, the value of that water goes up. If you survive a plane crash in the desert and have no water at all, the water becomes priceless to you. The more you have of something, the less valuable you find it. Basically, you take things for granted.

You are with yourself all the time. You can't escape. Ahhh! You have more of you than you know what to do with. Therefore, you tend to undervalue yourself. Small example: you probably have a smartphone. You use this digital appendage without even thinking. You just swipe your way to entertainment, information, and virtual connection. I doubt you've listed "competent smartphone user" as a skill on your resume. It goes without saying, right? Wrong!

My mom is a highly intelligent woman who has no grasp of technology. She calls me "tech support." When her phone was yelling at her about running out of cloud storage, I walked her through how to choose what she was saving to the cloud and how to buy more storage. We had a mini masterclass on what a cloud is. Y'all, I am not a technical expert, I'm just a millennial.

What are things about yourself you take for granted? These could be skills, but they can also be attributes or even quirks. I want you to write down at least three things about yourself that you've been taking for granted. If you can't come up with anything, start with the fact that you brush your teeth. Yes, teeth brushing is something we probably all take for granted. But think about what would happen if you decided to forgo this little morning ritual. Eek!

2.   Evaluate your measuring stick.

When we decide what we are worth, we usually do it by comparison. This is a normal way to establish a baseline value. We do it with almost everything. When you're buying a house, you look at comparable home sales in the area to decide how much to offer and whether or not that number will appraise correctly. Even when you buy pasta at the grocery store, you compare prices to make sure you're getting a good deal.

Remember that just because something is comparable doesn't mean its value should be taken as the final word. Your environment has a lot to do with this. Before I went to business school, I compared myself to my peers and the industry standards to determine how much my salary should be. After one week in class, I realized I was the least paid and lowest titled person in my cohort. I also realized I was not less intelligent, less hardworking, or less experienced than these people. My measuring stick changed. I knew that, even *before* I finished my MBA, I deserved a promotion and a substantial pay increase.

Who are you comparing yourself to? Are you comparing

down to people with worse circumstances? Are you comparing up to people with better circumstances? Comparison just creates a boost or a hit to your ego; it doesn't change your value. Your worth is not dependent on anyone else.

If you're going to compare (and you are) just make sure you're using the right measuring stick. Make sure you set your expectations based on your capability and not your circumstances.

3.   Decide for yourself.

The most important thing to take away from this chapter is that you should never let someone else's assigned value of you supersede your intrinsic value. Other people will try to tell you what you're worth based on your education, experience, skill, appearance, net worth, or relationships.[12] None of these things define your worth—they are just easy ways to compare you to other people.

How can such silly measurements define your true worth? How do you estimate potentzial? How do you measure the human spirit?

You can't. There is no way to put a number on the value of your life. There are two ways of looking at something with an undefined price: priceless or worthless. Neither has a measurable price attached to it, but their values are completely different. You are not worthless, you are priceless. Your value is too great to measure. There isn't a number that can do you justice.

So, the next time someone tries to tell you what you deserve (or don't) accept their viewpoint for what it is—an opinion. Opinions are not facts, so stop acting like they are. When people set limits on you, it's a reflection of their own insecurities and not your abilities.

CHAPTER 3

I Am Ruined

Trigger warning for sexual assault.
Please skip if you are uncomfortable with this material

MARCH of my sophomore year, my friends dragged me to a party at the boathouse on campus.

There are no boats at the boathouse, as far as I know, and you wouldn't want to take a dip in the water, because there's a running rumor about the parasite giardia growing in the depths. Regardless, there is an old wooden boathouse gracing the edge of the lake. Every Thursday night one of the popular clubs puts on a party in the upper rooms of the facility. The entry fee is five dollars or a case of beer if you're of age.

I wasn't a social outcast at school. I was just busy taking eighteen credit hours and working forty hours a week. So when my friends decided we were going, I took the night off. After all, I worked hard. It was time to play hard. We primped and then trekked our way to the thumping cabin. By ten o'clock, the place was raucous. We had picked an exceptional week to make an appearance, because not only was a beer pong tournament in full swing but also a DJ had created a dance floor in the second room upstairs. They had turned out all of the lights except for multi-colored Halloween decorations that must have been on sale at the local Walmart.

In typical female form, we entered in a pack of four, all dolled up and looking for the evening's finest Natural Lite and 90s music. We weren't disappointed. Natty could be found chilling on ice in any of the thirty-gallon trash cans strewn throughout. At a sophisticated southern women's college, you'd think we would have tea parties or wine *soirées*. Nope. A dirty boathouse with trash cans full of Natty was our delight. The entrance fee got you all you could drink until they ran out or the cops came, whichever happened first.

Beverages in hand, we headed for the dance floor. The night was dark and the room was even darker, but I could see that there were boys around. They usually bussed themselves in for our Thursday evening throwdowns. In the left corner by the door, there was a boy with a great mop of dark hair who stood about two inches above the crowd. He leaned against the wall and seemed to be taking in the room. Our eyes met, and he made his way to me. Of all people in the room, the mysterious tall boy with the surfer hair wanted to dance with me. My friends instructed me to "go get 'em, tiger" and let me be. We made small talk about this and that. I can't remember many particulars except that he was a fan of *Ghostbusters*, had an odd fixation on zombie movies, and had recently been asked by Hollister to be a store model. My nineteen-year-old self could not have been more impressed. Hollister was very cool. And a model (*swoon*).

The two (or three) beers I had drunk caught up with me; the night got a little fuzzy. I remember spending most of the evening with him. I remember making out on the back deck. I remember playing beer pong and embarrassing myself, because I am terrible at beer pong. Then it goes a little gray, but I do remember the cops shutting the party down. The next part I remember well. He hurriedly exchanged numbers with me so we could see each other again.

Squee! My little heart went pitter-patter.

Fast-forward to our next meeting, he wasn't quite as cute as he was in a very dark room, but he did have surfer hair and he was still into *Ghostbusters*, zombie movies, and, ostensibly, me. I didn't have any other romantic options on the table and after meeting his roommates, who were amazing, I decided I could keep seeing him. He was a terrible communicator, which surprised me since he was pre-law and kept droning on about how he was going into politics. Last time I checked, politicians were notoriously suave in their communication skills. Nevertheless, I looked past it. He brought me to parties on his campus and made sure we got in to see the good house bands. It was a nice setup. Looking back, the boys got in to see the good house bands if they had a girl with them (he went to an all-boys school). So, perhaps I was the good luck charm.

After about three weeks of dating, or talking, or whatever we were doing, it was my birthday. He was going to take me out to parties at frat circle, where all of my other friends would be. I thought it would be great to see so many friends in one place when I turned a decade older. The night started out fine, but my boo got into a spat with one of the fraternity boys and decided we were leaving. I would have preferred to stay, but you know, women acquiesce, so I went back to his dorm with him.

The dorms were set up so that two people shared a room, and the beds were lofted above desks. His was on the left side of the room. The room smelled like stale beer, cheap cologne, and pizza. A far cry from my scented candles and matching room decor. His roommate was out for the evening, so we had the place to ourselves. I thought I might get a nice "make-out" session in. I'm a huge fan of kissing, and he wasn't total rubbish at it. So we crawled up to the lofted space and did what college kids do best: attack each other's faces like there was no air left in the room. At one point he covertly unhooked my bra. I made some kind of "Oh, you've had practice" joke, to which he merely raised an eyebrow.

He asked if I wanted something special for my birthday. Now, I'm a good Christian girl and I'd had every kind of nonsex sex you can have while maintaining your virginity. He and I had already had the discussion about my commitment and he said he supported it. I said, "What did you have in mind?" He asked me to take my clothes off. So I did. He took his off too.

I took in all six-foot-something of him and kept on with the kissing, hoping I would get some oral sex out of the deal if I did a good job. He pushed me back on the bed and then hovered over me for a moment.

This is when I realized what was actually happening. He was not trying to give me a birthday treat, he was trying to fuck me. I pushed on his chest and said, "I don't think this is a good idea." He eased into me and whispered, "Shhhh," into my ear. I burned and stretched in ways I didn't know possible, and my eyes watered. Again I protested, "Babe, please, stop." He looked at the wall and started to thrust.

I went numb. I remember whimpering "no" and "please stop" so meekly I was nearly inaudible, but not completely silent. It went on for an eternity, but it finally ended with his climax and my tears. He left the room to wash up and I gathered my things and left.

Normally when I'm cornered, my fight instinct kicks in. This was not a normal situation. I ran. I put on my clothes. I ran to my car. I drove the hour home. I hid under my covers for three days. I didn't eat. I couldn't look my friends in the eyes, and I dodged phone calls from my family. I was so brutally ashamed I couldn't bear to look at myself in the mirror. I was disgusting.

The boy called three days later to break up with me. He told me he'd been doing some thinking and he wanted me to know I just wasn't quite good enough for him. He needed someone smart and beautiful and funny and fun, and I wasn't any of those things, but he wished me the best and hoped we could still be friends.

I thought it couldn't possibly get worse. I thought I'd hit the bottom, but that's when the floor caved in. Now I was a disappointment on all levels, and the thing I had been saving as a precious gift for my future husband was apparently garbage, because I was terrible at sex too. I was no good … at anything. Even the man who took my virginity didn't want the scraps he left behind.

The lie: **I am ruined.**

***

How I squashed the lie:

One in five women will be sexually assaulted during their lifetime.[13] That's more than a heartbreaking statistic, it's a life-changing statistic. Some people are assaulted by strangers, some are brutalized, some are attacked by people they know or care about. I wasn't raped in a dirty alley by a stranger, but my *no* was just as real, and the disrespect for my *no* was assault. That's present-day Nikki talking.

In 2007 I wasn't so clearheaded about what had happened to me. I thought if I had been stronger, if I had said no more forcefully, if I had been better, it wouldn't have happened. I was so ashamed.

Shame is a nasty visitor. For me shame felt like having a cannonball blown through my torso and then being covered in cement. Walking was hard. Breathing was hard. Eating was out of the question. Sleep was my only friend for a long time. I went through the motions of class, work, homework, but inside I was an empty husk. I have no idea how I got through finals.

One of my jobs on campus was in career services. I had two coworkers. One of them I loved, and the other one I could not stand. The one I didn't like was loud, overly talkative, and blonde. Kind of like a more obnoxious version of Galinda from *Wicked*. Everyone loved her except me—she wore me out.

To my great surprise, this flighty girl picked up on the fact that I was not okay. We went into one of the empty offices, and she asked if she could pray for whatever was going on with me. The wall holding back my emotions broke for a minute, and I burst into tears. She cried with me, listened to my story, held my hand, prayed for me, and never once pitied me. It was exactly what I needed. She invited me to her church and introduced me to her friends. It was not fast or easy, but I picked myself up off the floor, surrounded myself with people who encouraged me, and tried to leave the situation in the past.

But I was one messed up little lady for years. I would self-sabotage relationships because I was petrified that I was ruined. I rarely had a relationship that lasted longer than two weeks. Even if I liked the guy, I would get nervous that he would try to make a move and I wouldn't be able to stop it. If someone tried to kiss me on the first date, I'd duck and then ghost them. Once I became intimate with people again, I'd vacate my body until it was over and then turn over and cry quietly while the guy caught his breath. I got really good at hiding my tears.

Sexual penetration became incredibly painful for me. It took six months of physical therapy to get to a place where intercourse wasn't excruciating. My husband is probably the most gentle and generous lover I have known. Even though I'm much better, he still checks in with me to make sure I'm okay and that nothing hurts— every time.

I have experienced tremendous healing in this area of my life and want to extend my love and support to other victims of assault or abuse. You are not alone. You are not to blame. You are not ruined.

Here are some things that helped me along the way:

1.   I told someone.

Keeping this secret was eating me alive, and I didn't even know it. There is catharsis that comes from telling the truth, even when the truth sucks.

2.   I practiced kindness toward myself.

At the time making eye contact in the mirror was hard. So I started with just saying encouraging things to myself when I was alone. Eventually I got to a place where I could look at my reflection without instant nausea; this is when I had to be extra nice. My first instinct was to look away, or worse, pass judgment. That wasn't going to help. I had to actively replace the mean thoughts in my head with something sweeter and more forgiving.

3.   I surrounded myself with encouragement.

I only told one person what had happened to me, and she wasn't telling anyone, but I couldn't rely on her for everything. I found a group of snuggly people who were positive and encouraging. They had no idea I was dead inside or how much I needed their kindness. I will be forever grateful to the people who believed in me before I could face myself.

4.   I started helping other people.

This sounds impossible when you're in the thick of it, but I promise the fastest way to make yourself feel better is to fix someone else's problems. There are two reasons for this: you stop thinking about your own mess for a while, and you get good feels from being helpful.

5.   I got professional help.

Not immediately, although in retrospect that would have been a great idea. It took me several years to start going to therapy, and probably six months of sessions before I even started to dance around the subject of my assault. Listen, it was way easier for me to admit the problems in my family or at work than it was to talk about physical trauma. The therapist suggested alternate ways of looking at my situation and helped me stop equating the fact that I couldn't stop it with permission for it to happen.

***

How you can squash it too:

If you are the victim of trauma, assault, or any kind of experience caused by someone else's bad choices, you are not ruined. You are not alone. Your future is still there. It may feel so very far away, but I promise it's there for you if you want it to be. The hole in your chest will heal. The weight of depression will lift. The sting of shame will leave. You will get better. You just need to take a moment to find your footing.

RAINN, the Rape, Assault, and Incest National Network,[14] has suggestions for what to do after a sexual assault or violent incident. Their suggestions include talking to someone (their hotline, a psychotherapist, or friends and family); seeking medical treatment; setting up safety measures to protect yourself in the future; practicing self-care; and understanding that this is *not* your fault. Go to www.rainn.org for a plethora of information and support around this topic. If you haven't experienced sexual assault, I still think it's worthwhile to familiarize yourself with the statistics and learn how to become an ally to those who may one day need you. The RAINN website includes articles for people who are friends or family of sexual assault victims.

Psychology Today shares several types of trauma-focused therapy treatments for sexual assault victims.[15] These include cognitive processing therapy (CPT), prolonged-exposure therapy, and eye movement desensitization and reprocessing (EMDR). Each of these treatments looks different in practice but helps the individual work through the traumatic experience(s) and move forward in life.

You don't have to be strong for other people. You don't have to be kind to your aggressors. You don't need to forget it happened. You *do* have to forgive yourself. You are not to blame. Please take all the time you need to feel what you need to feel and do what you need to do (or not do) to take care of yourself.

Don't dodge it. According to Elyssa Barbash, in her article "Overcoming Sexual Assault: Symptoms & Recovery," in *Psychology Today*, "Avoidance is known to be the most significant factor that creates, prolongs, and intensifies trauma-reaction or PTSD symptoms."[16]

Practice self-care: physical or emotional. Physical self-care includes sleep, nutrition, exercise, and routine. Emotional self-care might include fun, a safe space or safe people, journaling, inspiration, and relaxation.

Don't set a deadline for recovery. I'm usually a big fan of deadlines, but this is an exception. You can't put a clock on your healing. It will take however long it takes. Be patient and be persistent.

Take control where you can. Sexual assault steals your power. It can make you feel out of control and overwhelmed. To take back some of that control, start small. Set small, achievable goals for yourself and meet them. This can be as simple as taking a shower or bath.

Reframe the situation. This does not mean ignoring or minimizing the incident. It is about finding meaning beyond it. You survived! What an unbelievable achievement. Not only did you survive, but you're going to live in spite of it. They took things from you, but they don't get to take your life, your future, or your hope. Those are yours.

The only way for you to ruin your life is to accept the lie that you've blown it and wallow in the pain. It's so easy to wallow. Way easier than picking yourself up and starting over. It's not better, though. I will never tell you to get over it. You don't get over assault. You decide that your life is not determined by someone else's mistake. You take back your life, but it is always a part of your story.

Healing is slow, but your life is not over.

CHAPTER 4

I'm Bad at My Job

HI, I'm Nikki and I'm a recovering perfectionist.

I am easily frustrated when things deviate from my beautiful plans. I feel responsible for things I have no control over, like weather, traffic, and other people. I like to be in charge. I can't stand when I'm not instantly good at something. And mostly I hate being wrong.

Intellectually I know that it is unreasonable to expect things to happen according to my timeline or desires. Realistically I always hope I've planned for every contingency and that this time will be different. This time it will be perfect. It rarely is.

A couple of years ago, I was hired to oversee projects that brought technology into our operations. This is a fancy way of saying I was helping people running the day-to-day business to be more productive by using technological advances such as automation, analytics, and artificial intelligence.

Small problem, I didn't know anything about our day-to-day business or those aforementioned technologies. No problem, I've started basically every job not knowing what in the world I was doing and always managed to figure it out … eventually.

This job was a little different. I walked to where my desk should have been and found someone else there. Not great. Apparently they changed my desk location and forgot to tell me. Minor inconvenience, I can roll with that. At my actual desk was just the desktop and chair. No monitors, no mouse, not even a spare pen. You are probably wondering why no one bothered to walk me to my desk or even set it up. Ah, well, that's because I was switching roles in the company and my new team worked in New Jersey. My manager told me to just hang tight and he'd call me as soon as he could. So I hung … for a week. In fairness, I tried to reach out to him each day, but got the brush-off.

Getting paid to sit in an office all day and do nothing isn't a bad gig, if you can swallow the guilt that comes with it. I tried asking for training materials or access to electronic filing systems where I could research what the team was working on. They didn't exist. There was no training.

I did get some busy work to do after that first week, but I didn't get assigned a project for nearly a month. This was a little problematic, since my entire purpose in this job was to manage projects. I was starting to second-guess my move, but the pay was really good so I stuck it out.

Fast-forward four months, and I was running three projects. I was never trained, but I was doing my very best to figure it out and work with my partners to ensure that everything stayed on the rails. Which is when everything went to crap. One of my projects just completely stalled, another tanked when our key contributors bailed for three months, and the last one proved that our hypothesis for how to make things better was never going to work. In addition to this, one of my project coleads told me that he was disappointed in my performance. He wasn't my boss, but he had a tremendous amount of experience so I took his opinion to heart. I again started to second-guess myself. I thought perhaps I was just really, really bad at my job, and they had made a huge mistake in hiring me.

The lie: **I'm bad at my job.**

* * *

How I squashed the lie:

I told you I hate not being good at stuff instantly. This was a double doozy, because not only was I not performing well, but I didn't know what I was doing wrong in order to get better. The only thing worse than doing something badly is giving up. There had to be a way to improve, and I was going to find it. I started by taking online courses on project management. This helped me understand what was expected from my role and how I could salvage my projects from the stinking pile of failure they were headed for. In my research I discovered that I had walked into the dumpster fire, not caused it. My colead was completely disorganized and never took the time to set up the projects correctly. So when things went bad, he found the easiest person to blame— me. I was new to the team, new to the work, and could not read minds. To be fair, I still can't read minds, and it still irritates some people (#sorrynotsorry).

My initial efforts in self-training seemed to pay off, so I continued the investment. I added listening to project management podcasts in the morning and networking with other project managers, both on my team and in other parts of the company. Four months later my colead was asked to leave the company and I was provided a new partner. In three months we had made more progress than the projects had seen in the year they'd been operational. The combination of my innovation, his untainted perspective, and our combined desire to finish produced massive results. Because of this turnaround, I was asked to lead a super-sexy collaboration project for the CEOs of two Fortune 50 companies. Not too shabby for someone who didn't know what they were doing.

My commitment to figuring it out and continuous improvement allowed me to lead that collaboration project with pizzazz. The topic of this collaboration was dental X-rays and machine learning. Another two things I knew nothing about, but I knew how to manage a project and how to go find information when none was provided. We had an incredibly tight deadline of eight weeks, and we nailed it. The team pulled together to deliver an outstanding presentation to the CEOs.

It's really hard to argue with results. I didn't have a great start in this career, but my mid-game was looking strong. I now believe that you aren't bad at your job unless your supervisor expressly tells you that you are not meeting expectations (with clear examples and suggestions for improvement). To avoid such conversations, I recommend setting up meetings with your manager or supervisor once a quarter to talk about your contributions, your career development, and their constructive criticism. These things will set you up for a thriving career instead of just leaving you to react to whatever your annual review has to offer.

* * *

How you can squash it too:

The thing about corporate America is that as far as teams go, you get what you get. Every time you take a new job, you roll the dice. Will the job description match the actual job? Maybe. Will the boss be a micromanager? Perhaps. Will your coworkers be cool? It's a gamble. Good training, good management, good teams, and good work are not guaranteed. Neither is your success. You are the master of your fate, as the British poet William Ernest Henley says. So you better figure out how to be a good one.

The good news is that you can do something about some of the things that make or break a good work experience.

Lack of Training

If your job provides the exact training you need, hallelujah. Do a happy dance and skip to the next section. If you received training that was subpar or nonexistent, there are a couple things you can do to help yourself.

1. Find someone who is really good at what you want to do and ingratiate yourself to them. Be their buddy and find out how they do what they do. Buy them coffee or lunch and ask all the annoying questions you can. See if you can sit with them and watch them work. Hang out in their meetings. Find ways to observe them (if possible) or have them coach you.

2. Ask for help. People tend to overestimate rejection and underestimate someone's willingness to help.[17] People are willing to help you, and they are even more willing to help when you make a specific request. You will be surprised by how helpful people are.

3. Read up on the internal company website and see what training or information is already provided. Sometimes there are vast troves of information just waiting to be found, but companies are notorious for crappy internal marketing of their training materials. If you work at a start-up or a small shop, this may not apply. I worked for a monster company and found hundreds of videos to watch about how insurance works. I won't claim the entertainment value or production quality blew me away, but I did gain a general understanding of what we did and how.

4. Take online courses. When I had exhausted my internal resources, I started taking online courses and reading books on my industry. Coursera and Udemy are great places to start looking. They do cost money, but they are reasonable compared to trying to get a new degree.

5. Listen to podcasts. There is a podcast for everything. So turn your morning routine into an educational experience. I started listening to project management podcasts and would pick up little tips and tricks while I was fixing my hair. It cost me nothing and was as complicated as doing a search in Apple podcasts for "project management" and hitting play.

6. Attend professional conferences and day or weekend seminars. I know going to seminars or conferences can

be intimidating if you're not extroverted. However, every time I go I come away having learned at least one new thing—usually more—and feeling more competent and inspired about my career. Plus you can do the dreaded N-word that everyone hates (networking), which could give you valuable friends and contacts who can help you in the future.

I'm sure there are a dozen other things you can do to make yourself better at your job, but those are the ones I used to train myself when training wasn't readily available.

Sucky Coworkers

This one is trickier. Coworkers can make or break a job, because you have to work with those jokers every day. Here are my tips:

1. Don't let anyone make you feel like garbage. I won't stand for it, and neither should you. Human turds do not wake up on their own and say, "Today I'm going to be less of a dick to everyone I work with." Nope, they probably think they are helpful, well liked, and sugar sweet. You have to stand up for yourself. If people are being mean to you, you have to tell them, nicely, that it's not okay and to please knock it off.

2. What if you have nothing in common with them? This one is probably more relatable. I have been the youngest person, the only unmarried person, the only female, etc. at a number of jobs, and it wasn't fun, but it was what it was. You can't change demographics, but what you can do is try to find common interests. It's not as hard as you think. You can start by talking about the weather, what's

for lunch at the canteen, or sports (if that's your thing). My best friends at work are people who, on the surface, have *nothing* in common with me. One of them is twice my age and loves dogs, two of them are moms to young boys, and one is a health nut, but we ended up finding common ground at work and now we have a monthly lunch club I absolutely adore. One of them was a bridesmaid in my wedding. Who would have thought?

3.   What if they're super negative people? Oh yes, we all know these types. They are rough, but if you're forced to interact with a negative person, you can make a game out of it for yourself by counting the number of times they complain and seeing if they break their own record (kidding). A better choice is to refocus the conversation around something positive and ask them what they want to do about the awful thing they are complaining about (this time).

Your Boss Sucks

Welcome to the club! High fives all around. Your boss could be unengaged, uninformed, unqualified, a dick, or just a complete nightmare. It's awful to have a bad boss, and mostly you're going to have terrible bosses. People are rarely going to live up to your expectations of them. There are dozens of books out there on how to deal with terrible bosses. What I can tell you is that being happy at work and successful in your career is your responsibility, not your boss's. In my opinion, you have three options.

1.   Manage up. Be the boss of your relationship with your boss and make it better. Make sure they know what you bring to the table and that you have access to the support

you need to be successful. Manage your career advancement too; don't expect your boss to tell you what the next move is or how to get there. You should start this dialogue and ask for their opinion on how to get where you want to go. You have to know what you want and make sure they know what you want.

2. Manage around. If you have done everything in step one and you feel like your boss is holding you back, you can go to the next level up from your boss (or higher) and ask for mentorship. Find a way to get your work seen by the right people, and take your career path into your own hands. Don't let someone stand in your way.

3. Get a new boss. You always have the choice to leave, but know that you need to do a lot of digging on the new boss to ensure they are the kind of person you want to work for. You don't want to end up in the same situation. I usually try steps one and two before I bounce.

Pro Tip: Keep a running list of all of your accomplishments throughout the year. Every time you do something cool, add it to the list. Try to do this at least once a month. You'll have ammunition for why you're a badass at the end of the year.

CHAPTER 5

I Don't Need a Backup Plan

I was in a multilevel marketing business for more than a decade. I promise you this is not a chapter recruiting you into any sort of direct sales company. I recognize that the spectrum of feelings about MLMs ranges from "key to my financial future" to "scam." Regardless of your feelings, please bear with me while I get to the point.

On a Tuesday night, a friend invited me to a marketing class in Lynchburg, VA. I was in college and currently taking a marketing class. So I thought I could swing some extra credit by going to a lecture in town. I walked into a large Baptist church and laid my eyes on more than one hundred people in business suits smiling and shaking hands. They warned me that the dress was business, but I didn't own a suit. I was wearing navy blue chinos and a nice white T-shirt—the nicest outfit I owned. I was instantly nervous, overwhelmed, and insecure about my appearance. My friend met me at the door and introduced me to at least fifteen people.

I can't overstate this enough: everyone was excited. They were excited to meet me, excited about the speaker, excited to see each other, probably even excited about my ridiculous chinos. I had a feeling I was in the wrong place. I'd been to business lectures before and no one was excited to be there, including the speaker. This was definitely not going to get me extra credit.

My friend walked me down the center aisle to the second row, first seat. Now, I grew up in church, and my favorite pew was any one that was not near the front. I felt completely exposed. The speaker got up on the small stage, and I swear he stared me down during the entire hour-long presentation. I don't remember all of what he said, but I remember him asking if I could use two hundred dollars per month. I was working five part-time jobs at school and making about two hundred per month. He said I could make a minimum of that working five to ten hours a week. This was easy math. For a quarter of the time that I was spending at my jobs, I could make the same amount of money. That's a better deal.

He asked if I knew six people who could use two hundred a month. I was a broke college student. Every single one of my friends could use that money, and there were more than six of them. After this he drew some circles, talked about the compound effect, and showed me that my two hundred could easily become two to three thousand per month. Cha-ching! I started spending that money in my mind immediately. I am gifted with good taste, and by good taste I mean the ability to find the most expensive thing in a store and fall in love with it.

At the end of his presentation, he pulled up twelve different people from the room and had them spout off their single best month in business. Some of these people were old, some young, some married, some single; one was in college. The smallest best month was nine thousand and the largest was over forty thousand. If those people could make that kind of money, I knew I could make two hundred a month, quit my campus and waitressing jobs, and focus on school.

I signed up on June 13, 2007. In July we went to a conference in Greenville, SC. There were over sixty thousand excited people in the coliseum. It was the most thrilling weekend of my life. I had found my calling. One of the speakers said he sold his 401(k) to fund his business and now he was a multimillionaire. Another speaker told me I didn't need a 401(k) if this was going to be my future. They told the story of Cortez burning his ships when he landed in America, so that his men had to win their fight with the natives. I got the message—401(k)s were an escape plan, and I didn't need any escape plan since I would have my own business.

The lie: **I don't need a backup plan.**

***

How I squashed the lie:

Two years later I was not financially independent, but I was graduating from college. So I found one of the only paying jobs available in 2009 and took it with a smile. I moved to DC with five hundred dollars in my bank account and tremendous expectations for the future. One small problem—I forgot to account for a couple of things in my paycheck. Little things, you know, like taxes, social security, and Medicare. I was an econ major, and it never occurred to me that the government took out social security *before* they gave it to you (*smacks head*). This wasn't a fun lesson, and I had to start cutting back on my spending. The company offered me 401(k) paperwork, which I promptly threw in the trash. First of all, I was going to be a successful network marketing superstar, not a corporate muckety-muck, and I did not need their escape plan. Second, like I had the money to contribute to that plan anyway. Pfft.

Five years later I still hadn't signed up for a 401(k). My business was fairly successful, but I wasn't making enough to replace my full-time income. I had every intention of never getting a 401(k) until I read *The Automatic Millionaire* by David Bach.[18] Bach talks about compound interest and the benefit to investing early. There was a chart that showed how small contributions early in life can lead to huge returns later on. Even if you made bigger contributions later, you'd never catch up to those who invested small amounts early.

Multiple streams of income are good! Not only did I know this but I regularly taught this principle to people. By not preparing for retirement early, I was actually losing thousands, maybe hundreds of thousands of dollars. All because I didn't want to invest a small portion of my paycheck in the present.

I set up my 401(k) before I left work that day. This was one of the best choices I have ever made. A couple of years later, my mentors in the network marketing business all but fired me. They couldn't actually fire me, but they did everything else in their power to tank my business. In twenty-four hours I went from having two hundred friends I saw twice a week, a thriving business, and credibility to having three friends in the world, no respect, and no hope for recovering my position. I wasn't just uninvited from events, training, and support. I was shunned. I watched as my dreams of the past twelve years went up in smoke.

Why did they do this? I was supposed to be working on giving more serious training talks, and I cracked two jokes at training the day before. My mentors pulled me aside and told me I couldn't follow a simple order, I was not liked, I was never going to succeed, I was mean, and my Christianity didn't stick. They accused me of actual demon possession and feigned concern over my immortal soul. I took a few deep breaths and calmly explained that they were wrong. Salvation isn't like sunblock; you don't need to reapply it. It's a one and done kind of decision. They insisted that I had to "get my life right with the Lord" and that I needed serious psychiatric help and medication. In addition to being demon possessed I was also (probably) insane.

I was used to them telling me I was a horrible person, but no one gets to question my salvation. I was pretty sure they were wrong about the possession and the crazy, but just to be sure, I talked to my pastor and sought out a psychologist. My pastor assured me that I was, in fact, still saved and not possessed by the devil. Phew. The psychologist assured me that I was nowhere near crazy nor did I need to be medicated—and that they had serious concerns about my mental health because of the level of emotional, spiritual, and verbal abuse I'd undergone for so long.

You are probably thinking this is a huge overreaction to cracking a couple of tasteful jokes. You would be correct. I'm funny, it's who I am, and I'm not sorry that I can make people laugh while teaching them something.

Even though my soul and my mind were proven to be sound, there was no going back. The veil was lifted and I couldn't unsee the ugly truth. My mentors were cruel, selfish people. My "friends" abandoned me without question. My dream was over, and I had to start from scratch to prepare for the rest of my life. Well, almost. I still had my day job and a 401(k).

Note: This story is my experience and one that is almost unheard of in the network marketing space. To my knowledge, I am the only person these people accused of possession and insanity. The parent company I worked for has no idea this happened and would likely be furious if they found out. That company never mistreated me or failed to deliver on their promise to provide me an opportunity and good products. Shoot, they were never even late with a paycheck. I am in no way trying to discourage anyone from building a network marketing business or following their dream. If you're out there networking your booty off, you have my utmost respect. I'm trying to make two points: (1) make sure the people who get a voice in your life are helping, and (2) there is nothing wrong with having a backup plan.

* * *

How you can squash it too:

Retirement is not age dependent. We spout off that retirement happens at sixty-five, because usually that's how long people need to save in order to support themselves without working. In America you become eligible for social security at sixty-two. Social security was never intended to be the primary source of your income in retirement. It's supposed to help supplement the lack of income from not having a job. If you want to retire, you need one thing: money. If you have enough money, you don't have to work anymore. You can do that at twenty-five or sixty-five, but you'll need more money if you want to retire early.

According to Kimberly Lankford, in her article "6 Ways to Prepare for Medical Expenses in Retirement," in *U.S. News & World Report*, "A recent study by Fidelity found that a 65-year-old couple retiring in 2020 will pay an average of $295,000 in health care costs over their lifetime, a 3.5% increase over the 2019 figures. That number includes Medicare premiums, deductibles and copayments, or coverage to fill in the gaps."[19] This number doesn't even touch your basic living expenses, travel, funeral expenses, or anything that comes up along the way. Most people assume they will have paid off their house, if they own one, by the time they retire. That cuts out the monthly mortgage payment, but doesn't get rid of utilities or property tax. The same goes for your car. If you pay off your car at sixty-five, you won't have a car payment, but you still have basic upkeep and taxes to take care of. Also, will you drive that car until you die? If you plan on kicking it at age seventy, the car will probably last you that long. If you want to live to eighty-plus, your car will be old and possibly falling apart. I'm not trying to scare you. You definitely don't have to work until you die. There are millions of ways to create ongoing income, including using a company-sponsored 401(k).

You can look up free retirement calculators online[20] and see how much you should be saving now in order to afford the retirement you want. I recommend thinking through how much money you'd like to have each month or year and adding in some unplanned expenses to the tune of at least 10 percent of your total annual income (roof replacement, new HVAC unit, bail money). Also think about planned expenses like insurance, travel, and

Christmas and birthday gifts for your family. Then take that amount and plug it into the online calculator to see what your numbers turn out to be. I do this periodically to make sure I'm still on track.

Regardless of where you are right now and how much money you have (or don't have) saved, it's a smart idea to plan for your retirement. If you have already started your 401(k) and you're maxing that bad boy out each paycheck, high five. If you haven't started saving for retirement yet, good news, today is the best day to start. Don't be discouraged if you look at the retirement calculator and it says you're behind. You can always catch up.

I heard a story on the radio once of a man who chose to live very frugally. He bought a small house and paid it off. He never went out to eat or took a vacation. He didn't have a high-paying job, but he invested a portion of his income each month for the future. Unfortunately he got very sick shortly after his retirement and passed away. He left over two million dollars to his alma mater.

There are two lessons here. First, there are ways to cut back on your living expenses today in order to fund your tomorrow. Second, don't *stop* living today because you're worried about tomorrow. We aren't guaranteed any tomorrows. Having a plan that accounts for both the present and the future will set you up to relish all of your days. You should enjoy every minute of your life now, but not at the expense of your future.

You can't go backward. I often wish I hadn't wasted so many years without saving for my future. But I can't change that. I can only do my best today and be consistent about it moving forward.

If you want to know more about saving for retirement, here are the books I've found to be most helpful:

- *The Total Money Makeover*, Dave Ramsey
- *The Automatic Millionaire*, David Bach

- *The Millionaire Next Door*, Thomas J. Stanley
- *I Will Teach You to Be Rich*, Ramit Sethi

Saving for retirement is not hard, it just takes a little discipline and maybe a slight modification in spending. With some planning you can work out a way to live your best life now and still be ready for your glorious golden years. The books I mentioned are great introductions to retirement planning, but feel free to consult a financial advisor to help you make a personalized plan for your life.

CHAPTER 6

A Bigger Weight Means a Smaller Life

I never struggled with my weight, like ever … until I did. And then it was all I could think about. I doubled my pant size in nine months. Most people didn't notice, because I gained it proportionally. I knew, though. I felt every single pound. I had to buy a whole closet full of new clothes—twice. When you aren't exactly flush with cash, this sucks with a capital S.

I've tried nearly every fad diet out there to get rid of this extra body weight. I've cut carbs, counted my macros, juiced, cleansed, ketoed, done Weight Watchers, fasted. I even tried to convince myself to develop an eating disorder (which lasted about four hours). Everything worked for a short period of time, but nothing really stuck. I'd lose weight and then I'd find it … and then I'd find some more. At my heaviest I put on nearly fifty pounds from my beginning weight. I'm five foot three, so every pound shows. When you're tall you can carry a little extra weight and no one can tell. For those of us who are more "fun size," five pounds looks like ten or fifteen. Fifty pounds is fifty pounds, though, and I did not feel good.

I love to work out, but I'm not one of those glamazons in the gym who can work out during lunch and come back looking beautiful and professional. I sweat like a pig. If you've gone to an unheated yoga class and seen the one girl dripping sweat onto her mat, it might have been me. It doesn't matter how in shape I am, I sweat just as much. If I go to the gym after work, I walk out looking like Alice Cooper with makeup running down my face.

Because I wasn't getting results with all the dieting and exercising, I did get checked out by a medical professional. I went to my primary care doctor and had labs run. I went to two other specialists, who checked for everything from thyroid conditions to rare diseases, to explain my weight. I saw a nutritionist, who made me write a food log for a couple of weeks and was blown away by how healthy I ate. The good news was that I am one healthy lady. The bad news was that I was still overweight with zero explanation for it. One of my doctors actually had the nerve to say, "You're fat, but you're a good fat. You're the healthiest fat person I've seen in a long time." Fantastic. I'm fit fat.

I thought I was doing everything I could to take the weight off, but it was freaking hard. In addition to feeling sorry for myself, I allowed my thoughts to run through worst-case scenarios for what would happen because of my weight gain:

- I was never going to find love.
- I wasn't going to move ahead professionally (the office where I worked only promoted women who looked like models—hand to God).

- I was never going to take the weight off.
- I wasn't pretty anymore.

The lie: **a bigger weight means a smaller life.**

***

How I squashed the lie:

When you don't feel good in your body, regardless of its size, it is exhausting. There is a nagging voice every time you look in a mirror, take a shower, get dressed, or try to do anything, really, that says, "You are fat and you can't do it." It adds stress to your already stressful life. In case you haven't heard, stress is a causal factor for weight gain.[21] I don't know about you, but when I get stressed out I eat. And I'm not talking about crunching on carrots. I usually grab something loaded with fat and carbs and comfort eat until I feel better and worse. Which is precisely how I gained weight in the first place.

Cheers to all my friends who have counted points or macros or calories and followed a grueling workout schedule in search of the perfect body. Who just knew that your new, hot bod was going to make that guy regret breaking up with you, get you noticed, make you Instagram famous, or allow you to finally stop worrying about how you look in clothes.

I've read a couple of dozen books on how to lose weight, and you know what the secret is? Eating right and moving more.

Annoying, isn't it? You know what I found worked best for me? This is going to sound woo-woo, but roll with me for a second.

Gratitude. You have to start with loving your body as it is and being grateful for what it *can* do. Show yourself some love for everything from your hair to your toenails. Be especially grateful for the areas you dislike most. Oh, you don't like your legs? I bet you like them better than not having legs. Think about how much more complicated life would be without legs. Same goes for every body part. Most of my extra weight collected in the middle. So I chose to be thankful for my gut and all of the necessary digestive and muscular functions they provide to keep me moving every day.

Here's what happened. When I started being kinder to myself and loving myself more, I realized I didn't need to look like those girls on Instagram. I didn't need fitness model abs to win a man's heart, or a perfectly peachy bum to get ahead at work. I realized I wasn't sixteen anymore and I didn't have to fit into the pant size I wore in high school, because I am a woman and I'm proud of my mature female shape.

Miraculous things started happening. I wasn't starving myself and then bingeing in secret. I didn't have to Grubhub guilty pleasure foods to my house and scarf them down before anyone got home. I didn't have to hide junk food at work. I realized that if I stopped denying myself and focused on taking care of myself, I stood a much better chance of feeling good, which is so much more important than a number on a scale.

* * *

How you can squash it too:

Your body is working so hard for you. You should take a few moments every day to show it a little gratitude and give it some grace. If this is hard for you, start with the parts you like. Maybe you have pretty eyes, a charming smile, gorgeous nails. Maybe you can be grateful that you have clear skin, that your hair is shiny, that your lips are pouty. Maybe you have full, womanly hips, strong arms, cute feet. I don't know, I haven't met you yet, but pick some things to be grateful for and work your way up to being grateful for everything.

In the same way we should not judge people by the color of their skin, we should not judge them for the space they take up in the world. I recently read a book called *Naturally Thin*[22] in which the author, Bethenny Frankel, proposes that a lot of weight gain comes from weight-loss attempts. Going on a diet can mess up your energy, fat storage, metabolism, and more. Dieting eventually ends and your body responds by trying to get back what it lost and then some. Not good.

We live in a culture obsessed with size. It will tell you that skinny equals healthy. I don't buy it. I want everyone to feel beautiful or handsome and confident at whatever size they are. I know this is not a current reality, but we can change the script, my friends.

When I was in high school, I wore a US women's pant size four/six and weighed 125 pounds. I was a year-round athlete and ate whatever I wanted. In Charleston, WV, the most popular store in the mall was Hollister. My four/six translated to an extra-large in shirts and a size twelve in pants. Both were the largest size Hollister carried. I was tiny, but was called "extra-large" and "biggest available" by a clothing store. They were telling me that if I gained any weight, I couldn't be in their club. What kind of message is this? What are we telling our children about what constitutes an acceptable body? It disgusts me. Currently the only thing that fits me from Hollister is the Malaia perfume and maybe some socks.

Do not let fashion dictate to you what is acceptable. It pisses me off that we are telling people you have to be a certain size in order to do anything. Like you don't deserve to eat if you don't fall into the standard-size clothing section of a store. That's bull. You deserve to eat and to live at whatever size you are. Can we stop judging what people put on their plates? I know people who are naturally thin and are accused of being bulimic because they eat a lot of food. I know people who are naturally heavier and are judged harshly for eating anything at all. This is so wrong!

I am all for changing things that don't make you happy, but I'm just as much for loving yourself where you are. If you want to make a change to your body, do it. Fluff up those curves, get the booty of your dreams, slim down if you want, get your swole on. Whatever it is, do it. AND love yourself exactly as you are today.

You are allowed to be loved, successful, and happy at any size, and don't let anyone tell you differently. Let's work together to overcome size prejudice. Let's normalize eating instead of dieting. Let's exercise because it makes us feel good instead of using it as punishment. Let's stop celebrating thinness as a virtue. Let us instead celebrate people for their kindness, confidence, natural gifts, and the goodness they bring into the world. Isn't that more important than their waist size? God, I hope so.

"Need" is a strong word. Do you really *need* to lose weight? I don't think so. I think you're awesome and beautiful just as you are.

I know you don't need to lose weight to find love, create a happy life, or get ahead professionally. What you do *need* to do is love yourself. Appreciate what your body does for you each and every day. Stop being Judgy McJudgerson for a minute and realize that you're an incredible person. So you're not perfect. So what? You know that no one else is either. Those movie stars and Fitstagram models don't even look like themselves IRL. Filters, angles, and Photoshop can completely change an appearance into something unattainable. Not only that but they are normal people with normal lives. They do not have their shit together, their parents drive them crazy, they've had crappy bosses, their kids are wild and dirty, their house gets messy, and they even occasionally eat cake (*gasp*). Personally, I find that more dessert in my life makes me happier than battling genetics to look like a size zero, but that's me. Do what makes you happy. And for Pete's sake, *please* allow yourself to eat, move in a way that feels good, and dress however you feel best without shame, guilt, or judgment. Your body is a gift, not a curse. Stop trying to wish it away. Embrace it.

CHAPTER 7

I Need to Wake Up Early to Be Successful

WHEN I finally decided that stewing in my depression and self-pity was no longer a viable option for dealing with my problems, I went on a mission to fix my life. It's not a secret that if you want something someone else has, you have to do what they've done. The only thing I knew how to do was build a network marketing business. That wasn't going to help me anymore, since I was blackballed from my own team. I needed to redefine what success looked like for me and study people who achieved those results.

At the time I had a massive Pinterest addiction. So that's where I started. I searched for success and success habits. I looked at the profiles of wealthy people and blog posts from average people who managed to make life look fun and exciting. I read books like *The Happiness Project* by Gretchen Rubin, *Smarter, Faster, Better* by Charles Duhigg, and *You Are a Badass* by Jen Sincero. In my quest to redefine success and establish meaningful habits, I saw a theme of people getting up early. Sometimes this was hinted at by an author's personal habit, but other times it was the premise of an entire article.

One such article is "This Is When Successful People Wake Up."[23] While Andrew Merle acknowledges that not every successful person gets up early, he also states that most of them do. He goes on to say that getting up early gives you a greater feeling of control over your day and access to the highest levels of willpower and productivity.

I wanted those things! I desperately wanted control, willpower, and productivity in my life. I wanted to give myself every advantage, and if that meant waking up earlier, I could do it.

I was going to wake up early (Rahhh! The crowd goes wild).

I was going to smash the shit out of my goals and create a life I loved.

I was going to get up at 5 a.m. and work out, read, make a healthy breakfast, meditate, write, make my bed, curl my hair, put on makeup the right way, get to the office early, and, and, and …

I hit snooze.

The lie: I need to wake up early to be successful.

***

How I squashed the lie:

It took about a month of me trying to get up at 5 a.m. and failing to realize that this was counterproductive. If you set and miss the same goal every day, you are doing twice as much damage, because now not only did you not do the things that were going to make your life better, but you added guilt to the equation. I did manage to get up at five once or twice, but out of thirty days, this wasn't impressive.

Last time I checked there were 168 hours in a week. Everyone has the same number of hours, regardless of their privilege, profession, or economic status. It's what I did with my hours that would determine my level of success. Time for some math:

- Ideally I'd sleep 8 hours a night (56 hours per week), and
- Work 40 hours at a job with an hour commute total and an hour for lunch (50 hours)
- Give myself time in the morning for dressing, eating, or just preparing for the day ahead (10.5 hours)
- Cook and eat a delicious dinner (7 hours)
- Workout 4 times a week plus drive time to the gym (6 hours)
- Spend quality time with my cats, friends, or partner (10.5 hours)

Add up all of that time and I had a grand total of 140 hours per week, with 28 hours free. That's more than one whole day open to learn something new, finish projects, keep the house clean, read, meditate, dance, build an empire, or hang out with family and friends. Whatever it is I wished I had time for ... I have it.

Even better, I found evidence that getting up early is not the be-all and end-all to living a successful life. *Harvard Business Review* wrote an article called "The Ideal Work Schedule, as Determined by Circadian Rhythms."[24] Their research shows that energy levels change throughout the day in accordance with a person's circadian rhythm (internal clock). Typically, people are most productive right after lunch and at 6 p.m. and least productive at 3 p.m. and 3:30 a.m. These estimates move up or down based on individual circadian rhythms. Early birds peak in alertness earlier in the day, and night owls peak later. Most people don't enjoy getting up before dawn or staying up half the night, and that makes them normal. The early birds and night owls are outliers.

The point is there is no best way to be. Whether you are working twelve-hour shifts, a typical nine-to-five, or a nontraditional schedule, you have to find what works for you and use your best energy when it's available.

Hallelujah! I did not have to continue torturing myself with a 5 a.m. alarm. I could be productive with a schedule that aligned with my body's natural rhythm and still get outstanding results.

***

How you can squash it too:

You don't have to get up at 5 a.m. to be successful. You just have to make the most of your waking hours. I'm giving you permission right now to set your own sleep schedule based on your goals, commitments, and circadian rhythm, and to never feel guilty if this schedule allows you to sleep in past ten or stay up past two. If you feel most engaged before the rest of the world wakes up, by all means embrace the dawn. But if the thought of a 5 a.m. wake-up makes you cringe, it's fine to pick a time that's more in line with your energy or schedule.

Regardless of your preference for wake-up times, I do recommend you take a full inventory of your time. If you're like me, it's often a mystery where the time goes. The easiest way to track down your secret free hours is to pay attention to what you're doing and how much time you're spending on it. If I'm not careful, all of my free time will go to Netflix instead of building my best life.

If you're a pen-and-paper person, you can either jot down start and end times for what you're working on or use a printable tracker from an internet search (image search "time tracking chart"). If you are more into electronic tracking, you can always create your own tracker in Excel or use an app. I've heard that Toggl Track, Harvest, and HourStack are good, but I have not used any of them since I prefer the handwritten way.

Once you know what time you have available, you can set some goals, break them down into daily activities, and schedule these around your commitments.

Goal Setting

If you want things in your life to get better, you have to first get very clear about what those things are and what better looks like. The easiest way I know to set specific goals is to use the SMART method:

- **Specific**: vague goals get vague results. You have to know exactly what you're trying to do. There's a difference between going to Raleigh and going to 235 S. Salisbury St, Raleigh, NC 27601. The first will put you somewhere in a city named Raleigh; the second will take you to lucet-tegrace, a delicious French bakery with killer macarons. Make your goals as specific as possible. An example of a specific goal is: I want to save an extra $8,492.63 to pay off my car.

- **Measurable**: this one is not a deal breaker, but it's helpful. If you want to get promoted to vice president of global operations at your company, your goal could be the amount of money you want to make in the position. If you want your business to grow in the next twelve months, you can measure profits, number of completed projects, or number of new clients. If you want to have a better relationship with your kids, you could measure the number of hours you spend with them each week or the number of cool adventures you take them on.

- **Achievable**: I will never tell you something is impossible, but make sure you aren't faking yourself out. Your goals should be something challenging but doable. If you currently can't swim, it's not a super great idea to sign up for the Ironman triathlon next month. Instead set goals to swim with your head in the water, swim a mile, or even just float without freaking out.

- **Relevant**: this should go without saying, but don't set goals you don't want to do. If you're going to take the time to achieve a goal, you should know why you want it. The why is more important than the goal itself. I set a goal once to get a computer programming certificate. I have zero interest in computer programming, but I wanted to make more money, and programmers have good starting salaries. The goal of learning to program was irrelevant and caused a lot of stress. I didn't like programming and I hated my classes. I quit after one semester. A more relevant goal was to get an MBA. I nerd out hard on spreadsheets, corporate strategy, and economics. My new goal was to get into and complete a top ten executive MBA program. Not only did I like the work, but I knew why I kept showing up. I completed the program in eighteen months and left feeling energized.

- **Time bound:** "A goal without a plan is just a wish," says author Antoine de Saint-Exupery.[25] Deadlines are important because they allow you to plan for the goal and make it real. If you try to set a goal without a deadline, chances are you'll procrastinate until it's no longer doable or relevant. When picking a deadline, make sure it's as specific as the goal itself. An example of a solid goal with a deadline is: I will be invited to speak at TEDx in Austin, Texas, by noon on December 31, 2021. Your deadline doesn't have to be that exacting, but it could be.

Chunking It Down

How do you eat an elephant? One bite at a time.

The same things applies to your goals. You can't expect your goal to manifest without intermediate effort. Even if you win the lottery you need to buy a ticket, watch for the winning numbers, and redeem the prize.

At Duke I had a team project that was worth nearly 50 percent of our grade. We had to do a strategic analysis of DSW, the shoe store. Examples of papers from the year before were twenty to sixty pages single-spaced. The professor warned us that we would not want to put off this project until the last minute. We would need to make consistent progress on a weekly or biweekly basis to not lose our minds at the end. Each lecture that semester was a topic that would be covered in the paper. Our program was set up so that lectures occurred every other weekend. We chose to take the week following each lecture to research and draft the corresponding section of the paper. At the end of the class, we turned in a forty-page paper and got an A. Other teams were not so focused. They tried to cram a semester's worth of work into the last week or two—bad move. They were stressed out, grumpy, and ended up with crappy grades.

Your goal is already measurable, so this part is just more math. Your goal will be 100 percent complete by your deadline. Determine what 50 percent looks like. Then break it down again— what does 25 percent look like? Keep breaking the goal down until you have something you can do on a daily or weekly basis that will move you toward the goal. These are your mini goals. You should set mini deadlines for each of them. For example: I want to add $10,000 in sales to my business over the next twelve months. This means I need to hit $5,000 in sales in six months. How do I do that? Each month I need $833.33 in new sales. That's $208.33 per week or $29.76 per day. Totally doable.

Time Management

Now that you have defined your main goal and supporting mini goals, it's time to take action. I find that it's helpful to set aside a specific time in your day for these activities. You may not know how long it will take you to accomplish your mini goal, but there's one way to find out. Estimate the time you think it will take, set aside that time in your schedule, and see if it was long enough or not.

Earlier in this chapter, we discussed what kind of free time you have, based on your normal activities. We found the free hours in the earlier exercise. Now we just need to turn that free time into goal-achieving time.

A good idea is to use some kind of planner or calendar to help you manage your time. Use whatever type of planner works for you: daily, weekly, monthly; electronic or paper. I have two paper calendars on my desk (and a titanic number of pen choices). One planner is weekly so I can see my commitments and goals at a glance, and the other is a daily planner to track my activities and priorities. I admit that this is overkill and slightly ridiculous. But it makes me feel good. So I'm going to keep on keeping on.

Start scheduling your commitments and your time for goal chasing. One of my colleagues has "Time for Learning" Fridays. He sets aside some of his free time on Friday to learn something new, since his goal for the year is to become better at his job and more knowledgeable in a couple of topics. If your goal is to meal prep for the week, block off the time in your calendar for when you're going to plan the meals, shop for the ingredients, and actually cook.

While you're in planning mode, it's a great idea to track your progress too. In the chunking phase, you set those mini deadlines. As you work toward your goal, you will begin to see how your progress is stacking up against your expectations. When you review your progress, you will know if you're on target or not. If you're behind, what can you do to be more productive? If you're ahead, you can either take a breather or you can keep crushing it and hit your deadline early. The best scenario is to be on time. If your goal was set properly, you will have to hustle to get there, but you can do it in the time allowed.

We have dispelled the myth that we must get up early in order to be productive and have instead identified how we can make the most out of the time we have. We did this by developing goals, breaking them down into doable steps, and scheduling those steps into our normal lives. As long as you know what you're working toward and have a plan for how to get there, you can maximize your energy spikes to help you achieve it.

CHAPTER 8

I'm an Imposter

IF you're thinking about an MBA now or in the future, do yourself a favor and check out Duke. They are top-notch. The courses are taught by world-class experts in their fields. You are surrounded by the best and brightest professionals out there. Staying on campus means roughing it at a five-star luxury hotel for the weekend. And did I mention the snacks? There are always snacks.

Duke is known for its academic prowess. You can't slouch your way in there. I think they keep the standards high because it proves to them you can hang with the workload. And work you will. There is no easy path to the end of the master's program. Also, they pump out class after class of ass-kicking business ninjas, most notably the CEO of Apple.

I got accepted in early 2018, and by May I was spending my first week on campus. I can still remember the rush of meeting two hundred new people, bonding with my teammates, and getting yelled at by the infamous Mark Brown. I was terrified, exhilarated, and a little confused by the yelling. It was awesome. I was not ready, but there I was doing the thing. For the next eighteen months, I was up to my eyeballs in study materials at any given time. Between terms we would get a couple of weeks to breathe. During that time I checked out of my adult life and went into professional couch potato mode. I showed up at work (barely) and then went home, ordered food, and watched Netflix until my eyes bled (#selfcare).

The thing I remember most vividly from my whole experience, besides the snacks, was week three of every semester. I get super excited about school and new classes. I love to start my semester strong by doing all of the prereading and assignments. I buy new highlighters and notebooks so that I can bring my A game to class. I'm a shameless nerd. But by the third weekend of class (out of six), I would hit a wall. Assignments or tests would pop up and I would suddenly discover that I was not good at this class. I was, in fact, not good at any class. I had no idea what I was doing and was going to fail out of a top ten MBA program. This didn't happen once. It happened Every. Single. Term. For Every. Single. Class.

At this point I would start asking myself what the hell I thought I was doing. There was no way I was going to make it to the end of that term. I was going to embarrass myself and others with a glorious flameout. I'd start to think I should just quit and save myself the effort of continuing.

Enter imposter syndrome: the feeling that I would be exposed as a fraud. It's a nasty bugger. I constantly doubted my accomplishments despite the work it took to achieve them. I would question my capability, success, and self-worth. I didn't let it knock me off course, but I did let it make me feel like my achievements were worthless. Oh sure, I did the grueling work, but other people did it better or easier, so their work was superior to mine. I was damned if I did and damned if I didn't.

The lie: **I'm an imposter.**

***

How I squashed the lie:

Imposter syndrome is a downward spiral. For me it started early in a project when I was defining my goals. A niggling insecurity about my ability to achieve the goal whispered, "There's no way," into my ear. I usually combated this with frantic planning to over-compensate for the doubt. I convinced myself that if I had normal plans, stretch plans, and contingency plans for this project, there was *no way* it could fail. It usually didn't, because I'd planned the thing to death. When I did achieve the goal, I couldn't allow myself a moment of celebration, because I was already feeling guilty about doing the thing in the first place. I must have gotten lucky. Other people didn't have to work as hard for it, so their success was better than mine. It was a better win if they didn't have to suffer as much. So to make myself feel better, I set new goals—usually bigger ones—and the cycle started over.

There's a reason they call it a syndrome, folks; it's clearly a sickness.

Valerie Young, author of *The Secret Thoughts of Successful Women: Why Capable People Suffer from the Impostor Syndrome and How to Thrive in Spite of It*, identifies five styles of imposter syndrome:

1.   The Perfectionist

Perfectionists hold themselves to the highest standards. They believe that not only do they have to do difficult things but they must do them without any mistakes. A mistake, setback, or failed achievement is taken as a personal reflection of their character and ability. They are rarely satisfied with their work; even when they hit their goals they believe they could have done it better.

2.   The Superwoman/man

These are your basic overachievers. It's not good enough to master a single area of their lives, they want to be brilliant at everything. They don't allow themselves to be average in any way and will push themselves to unhealthy limits to ensure they can do it all. They have to be constantly striving for a goal. It's actually stressful for them to relax.

3.   The Natural Genius

These people are quick studies. They can easily develop acumen. They were the people who didn't have to study in class to get an A. Because most things come to them so effortlessly, they feel like something is wrong if they have to work hard. They expect that everything should be easy, and if it's not they have failed.

4.   The Soloist

You know how toddlers go through a phase where is everything is "I do it myself!"? The soloists never really get past this. For them, asking for help shows weakness and failure. They feel responsible for every part of their accomplishments and will refuse help. Even if the help would get them to their goal faster or produce a better result, they believe it nullifies their efforts and shows incompetence.

5. The Expert

Experts are detail-oriented. They have to know everything before they can start. They always seek out information on how to do the task better. However, they fall victim to the old trap of paralysis by analysis. If everything isn't perfect or there are still unknowns, they can't move forward. They would be mortified to not be able to answer every question, meet every requirement, or have the best plan.

I can be all of these imposter types, but the ones that bug me most often are being a soloist and a natural genius. I have it baked into my brain that all of my efforts should be immediately successful without any help. I know intellectually that people who are best at what they do have to work at it, but because I learn so quickly it seems like my path to mastery should be short. When I'd hit that point midsemester where I had to work at learning, I got frustrated. Because I had to study to understand, I felt like I was stupid. When it took me several attempts to get something working I felt like I didn't belong.

So, I (*gulp*) reached out for help. I got myself invited to a study group for local students. Every student in that group struggled with at least one concept over the course of our time at school. Yes, even the ones who were probably actual geniuses. Before I joined the group I had no idea anyone else felt insecure about their work.

Our class was made up of fast learners. Fast learners are often christened as smart kids, because they pick things up quickly. A normal learning environment accounts for all rates of learning and moves at whatever pace works for everyone. In an eighteen-month executive MBA program, the pace doesn't work for everyone—it's breakneck. Even fast learners don't get any breathers.

Realizing I wasn't alone took the edge off my anxiety. Leaning into the concept of teamwork not only reduced my stress but improved my performance. That realization was worth the entire price tag of my MBA. For the first time in my life, I realized that everyone has strengths and they are all different. When you work together, you get to support the team where you are strong and also get supported where you are weak. The result is more creativity, better quality, and more time to focus on what you do well.

I no longer felt like I was an imposter, because I broke some of the bad habits that kept me in that cycle. When I did hit submit on that final project in my last semester, I wondered why I ever doubted myself in the first place. Also, I popped a bottle of prosecco and danced around my house.

* * *

How you can squash it too:

All of types of imposter syndrome hold you back. They can cause anxiety, depression, self-doubt, physical problems, or relationship problems. Basically, it's not healthy or productive. You can combat this insecurity in a few ways.

1. **Allow room for mistakes.** Les Brow, renowned motivational speaker, says, "Anything that's worth doing is worth doing badly until you get it right."[26] There is no straight line to success. It will take a series of course corrections to get where

you want to go. This is not shameful. In fact, it is probably more helpful to you long term. By knowing what won't work, you can more easily identify what will work.

2. **You don't have to do it all.** Duke's entire program is based on a team approach. Until that point in my life, I had done everything as an individual contributor. I lived alone and worked in a silo. If something was going to get done, I had to do it myself. This is a selfish and stupid attitude. I found out by working in teams that my way was not always the best way. Leaning into the teamwork got me better results, taught me new ways to do things, and removed a ton of stress. I was able to capitalize on other people's strengths in areas where I was weak. I was able to lean on people for support when I didn't have the time or energy. I did do it all, but I did not do it alone. Being superhuman is exhausting. Working with other people doesn't detract from your own accomplishments. It allows you to do more, do better, and improve your relationships.

3. **Hard doesn't mean bad.** Some things are going to be a breeze for you. You will enjoy the work and virtually sleepwalk your way to victory. That's not everything, though. Sometimes what you want to do is outside of your skill set or comfort zone. That doesn't make the effort any less valuable. It means that you have to knuckle down and work for it. There is no shame in hard work. People who are the best at what they do have had to sacrifice, hustle, and grind it out until they became great. You don't wake up one day and qualify for an Olympic team. You have to practice. The Olympic judges don't care if you have to work half as hard or twice as

hard as everyone else to master your sport. They only care if you can rise to the occasion when it's your turn to perform.

4. **Don't die in the details.** I'm a big-picture person, so this one is easy for me. My husband, however, is deeply concerned about details. He needs details on the details. When we first started dating, I invited him to come with my family to Hawaii to see my sister get married. It took him seven months to agree to come. He needed to first budget for the plane ticket, understand what we would be doing every day of our trip, take a week off work, and understand where our relationship was going before he could make this decision. It frustrated the tar out of me and led to our first argument. Are the details necessary? Sure, but don't let them take over your life. Don't miss opportunities because you don't have all of the information.

5. **You don't have to have all the answers.** Similar to dying in the details is feeling responsible for them. You are allowed to not know things. You are allowed to go find the answer and get back to people. It doesn't make you unqualified, it makes you human. However, if you figure out a way to download Google to your brain and know everything at once, please let me know.

6. **Own your accomplishments.** It's easy for people with imposter syndrome to own their mistakes. Usually, mistakes are just evidence of why you don't deserve whatever you're trying to do. What you need to take ownership of is your accomplishments. You did a thing! That is badass. Take a moment to revel in your own awesomeness. You deserve it.

7. **Feelings are not facts.** Just because you feel unworthy does not make it true. You are entitled to all of your feelings,

the good ones and the bad ones. Just don't allow those feelings to hold you back from your potential.

If you start to feel like you don't deserve what you have (your house, your family, your finances, your job, your reputation) I will challenge you to think back to all of the effort you put in to get there. I believe in luck, but I believe it's a sister to qualification. If you feel like you don't deserve to be there, know that you have been chosen for that specific role. God, the universe, fate, whatever you believe in, has chosen you to have what you have. Now is the time to show gratitude for the opportunity by doing the best you can. Beating yourself up won't make things better.

You are capable of big things. You deserve success, happiness, and an incredible future. Don't shortchange yourself.

CHAPTER 9

Everyone is Moving on Without Me

THE internet is a wonderful and terrible thing. In the age of social media, we are constantly exposed to the highlight reel of everyone's lives. People post about their perfect marriages, angelic children, new stuff (home, car, shoes), epic vacations, massive accomplishments, new bodies, promotions … it's exhausting to keep up with it all. When I measured my life against everyone else's, I found my circumstances severely lacking.

I don't want to give social media all the credit. I can play the comparison game anytime, anywhere. Everywhere I looked, I saw what I couldn't have. I'd go to work and see other people getting promotions. Yet there I was, making even less money than I did at my first job and getting passed over for opportunity after opportunity. I'd go home and my roommate would be out with her boyfriend—reminding me that my romantic life was a disaster. Her absence was ever so slightly less offensive than getting on social media and being overwhelmed with engagement and wedding photos. My life plan dictated that I should be getting married at twenty-seven and starting a family at thirty. I couldn't very well do that if I was getting ghosted by loser number two for the week.

I was working out like my life depended on it, only to find that my abs were still (mysteriously) in protective custody. When I'd show up to the gym, the bunnies would parade half naked through the weight room, flaunting their tiny waists and perfect hair. If people weren't getting sexy, promoted, or married, they were traveling to exotic places. I don't mean to brag, but the most exciting place I went that year was Aurora, Illinois, for a business conference. There's nothing wrong with Aurora except that it isn't Tahiti. How come I was the only person stalling professionally, personally, and spiritually?

The lie: everyone is moving on without me.

***

How I squashed the lie:

Over a period of a couple of months, I followed this car wreck of a story on Facebook. A girl I knew who usually flooded my news feed with cutesy couple photos suddenly changed her name back. She married her high school sweetheart, and they had what appeared to be a nauseatingly perfect relationship. It was a prom-queen-marries-football-star situation. They were the popular couple who found real love in their teens and got married at the first opportunity. Then out of nowhere, she showed back up in my news feed sporting her maiden name, and her relationship status was missing. (*steeples fingers*) Interesting.

No one ever came out and said what happened, but there were enough comments, photos taken down, and status changes to infer the gist of the story. She cheated on the perfect husband. *Dun dun dunn.* A couple of months later she was sporting engagement photos with her new fiancé. I was so pissed that she got to get married twice while I was still out there in singles land digging through a mountain of bad dates for a boyfriend. Then it happened. She posted about her new baby. Aha! The prom queen didn't have people lining up to marry her; she got pregnant with another man's baby while married.

That's when I really, really wanted to be small, petty, and proud of myself, but I stopped dead in my tracks. Three people's lives were probably ruined by bad choices, and I was about to have a party? What kind of monster was I? I immediately reevaluated my perspective and found it in need of a shift.

Things online aren't always what they seem. Everyone knows that, but this situation brought it home for me. I used to ask, "How come this isn't happening for me?" which places the blame for any lack in my life elsewhere. I made it someone or something else's fault that my life wasn't going the way I had planned.

Now when I see someone else's happiness, three things happen:

1. I ask myself if it's something I want.
2. If it is, I come up with a plan to get it. If it's not, I let it go.

3. Whether or not I want what they have, I give the person full credit for earning something good and send them my love. I don't have to have everything everyone else has.

A couple of months ago, I saw an update from a high school friend's little sister. She sold her book to a publishing house. I could have decided I was a writing failure because someone younger than me got to my dream first. I didn't. Instead, I was proud of her for doing something hard and asked for her advice on how to do it. She was more than happy to share some tips. I look forward to seeing her at book conventions and thanking her for encouraging me to finish strong.

People will continue to live their lives regardless of how it makes you feel. You do not get to decide how much happiness or success they deserve. You are only allowed to decide how much happiness and success you deserve.

***

How you can squash it too:

I can't tell you to stop comparing yourself to others. That's not realistic. Comparison is a natural way to analyze differences. When we compare, we have no problem being fairly objective and mentally stable. You compare prices, features, and produce without initiating toxic thought patterns. The difference is that we go a little nutty when we compare someone else to ourselves. Then it becomes a personal attack. Only we are the ones doing the attacking.

Here are some ways to deal with comparison:

1. **Keep your eyes on your own paper.** No, I mean it. If you can't be happy for someone else's happiness, stop looking at it. Focus on yourself, your goals, and what you need to do to create a life you love. If this means taking a hiatus from social media, so be it. Your situation is different and you don't get to have what someone else has just because it looks good. You are charting your own course and need to stay focused to get where you want to go.

2. **Knock it off.** When you feel that twinge of jealousy or haughtiness start to rear its ugly head, acknowledge the feeling and then tell it to go away. Only make room in your life for things that are helpful. You are so much better than being petty.

3. **Show a little gratitude.** Instead of worrying about having/being/doing more, take a few moments to reflect on what is already good. Take an inventory of your own achievements and show some gratitude for whatever helped you get them. Author Roy T. Bennett says, "If you aren't grateful for what you have, what makes you think you would be happy with more?"[27] Sometimes we need do stop and focus on what's already good instead of searching for what might be better. There is no guarantee the other thing *will* be better, anyway.

4. **It's not a competition.** Someone else's success does not take away from yours (#facts). You are allowed to choose your own adventure and love every minute of it. I highly encourage you to quit worrying about what other people are or aren't doing and focus on yourself. Good things are not always going to happen to you before they happen to anyone else.

5. **Use jealousy as fuel.** People do cool shit all the time. I am
    constantly inspired by the creativity, dedication, and stunning
    performances out there. When you see something that makes
    you jealous, swap it out for inspiration. Being inspired is a
    much healthier space to work from. Besides, they just showed
    you that your dreams are possible.

6. **Realize you don't know the whole story.** You don't
    know everything someone did to get what they have. So you
    can't feel discouraged by not getting the same results. They
    are human, just like you, and had to do something to get what
    they have. It doesn't mean you can't do it too; it just means it
    happened for them first.

7. **If you really want what someone else has, go get
    it.** There is no law out there that says if someone else finds
    happiness, you are doomed to misery. If someone else finds
    love, you are doomed to loneliness. If someone else gets a
    good result, you might as well stop trying because all the good
    is gone; there's nothing left for you. That's ridiculous and you
    know it. If you want the same outcome, prepare to put in the
    same effort. You can have anything you want in life if you're
    willing to do something about it.

    Comparison is the root of all evil. Somebody somewhere is
going to live your dream, but that does not mean you can't do it
too. You are capable and worthy of living the life you've dreamed
of—you just have to make it happen. Success and happiness aren't
available in limited quantities. If you want what someone else
has, chances are you'll have to do what that someone else did to
get there. There's nothing wrong with wanting a life that looks
completely different from anyone else's, either. Happiness is a state

of mind. Spend more time focusing on what's good and dreaming of what could be better.

You're not falling behind. This isn't a race. Getting there first doesn't matter as much as finishing. You don't know who is waiting for you to achieve your own goals. Go out there and make them happen.

CHAPTER 10

Love Will Solve All of My Problems

I have been on more than fifty first dates in my life. Like the movie but without the amnesia and with different people. I'm not particularly proud of this, but it happened. Any recommendation for how to find love, I've done it. I've done the apps, been set up, dated coworkers, dated friends, met strangers at bars …

I thought that once I found love, my life would be complete. I was wrong. I've been in love about half a dozen times. In a select few instances, my partners loved me back. In a couple of instances, they barely knew I was breathing. Usually it was something in between.

The first time I fell in love, it was intense. On my first day as a lifeguard, before the pool even opened, all of the staff had to show up and help clean the facilities. The pool is only open between Memorial Day and Labor Day; it spends the rest of the year getting grody—leaves, spiderwebs, dirt, dust, algae. We swept and scrubbed until we were blistered and aching. Halfway through that day, I saw a skinny boy with luscious brunette locks scampering across the far side of the pool deck. My heart stopped beating. He turned near the diving board and the sun caught his piercing blue eyes. I was done for. I didn't know his name, but I knew this was the man I was going to marry.

Once I found out who he was, I did everything in my power to woo him. By this I mean I requested to work on the same days he did. I brought him breakfast. I washed his pool laundry. I did his chores (in addition to mine) so that he could leave early. I stared longingly at him until even I knew I was being creepy. I started listening to '80s hair bands and would blast them as I pulled into the parking lot so he knew we had the same taste in music. Shock of all shocks … this method of wooing did not work. Over the course of three years, he proceeded to date every single female lifeguard except me.

He graduated a year ahead of me and went to college, still dating one of our coworkers. By December they were engaged. I cried for two weeks straight. I mean big boo-hoo tears bursting from my face at a moment's notice. I LOVED him and he was going to ruin our lives by marrying someone else. If you think this is ridiculous and pathetic, you are right. When he called off their engagement a couple of months later, I recovered from my depression.

I went home for fall break my freshman year of college and posted on Facebook that I wanted to catch up with anyone who was available. That boy was available, and he wanted to see me. My heart sang (*cue angelic harmonizing*). Maybe this was the night he'd realize he was secretly in love with me too! He was dreamy as ever, and we had a really fun night. When he kissed me, my knees actually gave out and I collapsed onto the wall behind me. This happens with extreme buildup sometimes. Your body can't handle the joy and just collapses.

That was it, though. I went back to school and we never hung out again. I do keep tabs on him from time to time, and he is married. Unfortunately, he grew out of his good looks and lost all of his hair. He has an average job at an average company and appears to be happy living an average life. I was wrong; we were not soul mates.

The next time I fell in love was with a woman. We had a hot and heavy long-distance romance that lasted a couple of years. I planned my entire day around when I could talk to her. I spent all the money I didn't have buying a plane ticket to see her. I wrote her songs on the piano. These I never played for her (thank God). The few times we got to be together for a weekend, I could hardly let her out of my sight. I was like a desperately dehydrated person near water for the first time. I couldn't get enough of her. When I went home, I was inconsolable. For weeks I was depressed and weepy. That last Christmas together, she told me I needed to get my life together, because she was going to marry me one day. I believed her. This was before it was legal for two women to marry. I didn't care. I was in love.

Eventually the distance got to be too much, and we called it quits. Several years later she married someone else. Even though I had moved on and was in a fairly stable relationship, I was still a bit shocked that she'd done it. I had thought that when she said she wanted to marry me, she meant it, and that someday, somehow we'd find a way back to each other. Nope.

I fell in love a couple more times and always thought I'd finally nailed it. I'd cracked the secret love code and would be fulfilled and happy for the rest of my days. Each time I was wrong.

Eventually I'd start dating again, and if I didn't have a setup or someone in my network worth pursuing, I'd reinstall my online dating apps. According to eHarmony[28] 40 percent of Americans use online dating services. People in every age group are migrating to these services, but the largest group of users is still eighteen-to twenty-nine-year-olds. Surprisingly, slightly more men than women are on these social platforms, and they say they don't get enough ~~attention~~ messages.[29] I thought it would be easy to find a partner this way, since the odds were in my favor. I tried everything from eHarmony to OkCupid to Christian Mingle to Tinder.

eHarmony told me, after I filled out their ridiculously long matching survey, that I fell into the small percentage of their applicants who couldn't be matched. What the heck? No lie, they wouldn't help me. Christian Mingle was probably the biggest disappointment. First, the pool of candidates was dramatically smaller than any other site, and second, the few decent choices never responded. Maybe I was coming across as too forward and not submissive enough by messaging them first. Tinder and Bumble went pretty well for a while. There seemed to be a ton of decent options, and no one sent me pics of their junk (so grateful). I can't say if it was me or them, but nothing ever went past a second date.

I thought if I just kept trying, it would be statistically impossible for me not to find a compatible match. It was a numbers game, right? Once I went on enough dates, I'd find someone who wanted a relationship and then, boom, my life would be perfect.

The lie: love will solve all of my problems.

* * *

How I squashed the lie:

Dating became exhausting. It was the same thing over and over and it led to nothing. I would scroll the options and swipe. I'd get a match and then do the weird "how do we start this?" dance. I have to admit, my pickup lines were never impressive, but some of my matches were clever. One of them commented on my Wizarding house (Ravenclaw) and said that he was a Gryffindor, but he wanted to know if I would let him Slytherin. It's so bad it's good, right? I wasn't looking for a good time. So even though it was funny, I had to pass.

Conversations would either sizzle or fizzle, and once or twice a week I ended up on a date. I'd agonize over what to wear, spend way too long fussing with my hair, and arrive early, only to sit in my car and wait for a more appropriate time to show up. The dates were rarely bad, but they weren't giving me butterflies. I'd come home and complain to my friends that the dating pool was awful, it was so hard to find good chemistry, and I didn't understand what I was doing wrong. They would try to comfort me by agreeing that dating sucks and then telling me I was trying too hard. The resounding suggestion was that I stop thinking about it and just "let it happen." Right, like Cupid's arrow was actually going to strike when I least expected and I'd turn around and face my destiny? Doubtful. I just had to work harder.

Then I hit a slump where I went on something like ten underwhelming dates in a row, culminating in a second date during which the guy attempted to physically force himself on me. Been there, done that, did my time in therapy—no thank you. I pushed him back hard, which threw him off balance and gave me enough time to grab my keys and bolt. That was the end of my online dating career.

I sobbed to my best friend that love was a lie and I was giving up. Instead of arguing with me and trying to restore my faith in humanity, she said, "You're right, and I think giving up is the right move." What? She gave me a pep talk, but it wasn't the one I wanted. She told me that I was trying to make every person THE person. I was giving them permission to control my entire happiness, and it was too much to ask for. I had to stop waiting for my other half to show up and become a whole person on my own.

I was contorting myself into whatever I thought someone else wanted instead of looking for someone to complement who I already was. Someone else was not the answer. I had to figure out who I was, what I wanted, and how to be content.

So I gave it all up—the dating, the trying, the expectations. I worked on being what I needed instead of what someone else wanted. I took myself on dates, played jazz music while I cooked, made a point of trying new things and allowing myself to not like them. I became the support system I was looking for, and it felt really good. There's a lot of acceptance, forgiveness, and self-care that goes into loving yourself; I highly recommend it.

When I decided to become a whole person and stop looking for my missing piece, I was able to bring a better version of myself to my relationships. I became more attractive to people because I removed the pressure for them to make me happy. My friendships got more fun. My family bonds strengthened. Even my work relationships improved, because I became a real person who could make her own contributions and have opinions. I even became more attractive to romantic partners, but I also became more selective.

My husband has a lot of great qualities, but my favorite two are that he doesn't rely on me to make him happy and that he is willing to dig in when things get hard. Love is not just a feeling. It is a verb. It is a choice, and not a choice you make once. You have to keep making it.

* * *

How you can squash it too:

You need relationships in order to be happy, but not necessarily a romantic one. Authors Emily and Amelia Nagoski say it this way:

> No one is "complete" without other people—and we mean this literally. To be complete without social connection is to be nourished without food. It doesn't happen. We get hungry. We get lonely. We must feed ourselves or die. We don't mean you "need a man" or any kind of romantic partner. We mean you need connection in any or all of its varied forms. And it is also true that the lifelong development of autonomy is as innate to human nature as the drive to connect. We need both connection and autonomy. That's not a contradiction. Humans are built to oscillate from connection to autonomy and back again.[30]

If the Covid pandemic has taught us anything, it's that life in isolation is not as fun as it was before. Even extreme introverts are finding they miss the hubbub of daily life. While you are working on embracing and nurturing your social relationships, I want you to embrace and nurture yourself. Loving yourself will allow you to show up more authentically and powerfully in everything you do.

Here are some things that helped me:

1. **Take responsibility for your own happiness.** My mom often tells me that it's my responsibility to "fill my own cup." She's right. No one is going to keep your cup full but you. Also, you can't pour anything out of an empty cup. So you must love yourself before you can effectively love others. It's not fair to ask anyone else to take ownership of your happiness. You need to figure out what makes you happy and do it.

2. **Get comfortable doing things alone.** I was petrified of doing things by myself for years. I would skip meals in college if I didn't have a friend to eat with. The only way to get past this one is to just do it. Take yourself on dates. No one is looking at you and thinking, *Oh, that person is so sad because they are eating alone.* People in Target are not looking at you and saying, "Yep, there's something wrong with that person because they are shopping by themselves." No one cares. They are too wrapped up in their own drama to worry about yours. And if they are thinking those things, shame on them. They should work on self-love and go on a solo date.

3. **Decide who you want to be.** Instead of waiting for a relationship to fulfill you, decide what you need in your life, what you can live without, then fill your own gaps. I needed to become my own biggest cheerleader. I wanted to do big things, and I knew that I had to become my own support system. I also had to become my rock. When things went terribly wrong, I needed to be okay. I had to learn to live without dumping on people. I'm not saying I never vent—I do—but I don't expect other people to fix my problems for me.

4. **Love your best parts.** Take an inventory of everything that makes you proud of yourself. Love those parts of you. It's not conceited, it's healthy. You will be able to live and grow without external validation, because you will value yourself.

5. **Love your worst parts.** Same thing. Take an inventory of everything that disappoints you about yourself. Good, now choose to love yourself anyway. How can you expect other people to love your dark parts if you don't love them?

The point is, you can be happy, fulfilled, and successful without a romantic partner. You can also be happy, fulfilled, and successful with a partner. Either way, you have to learn to be happy and love yourself. If no one has told you lately, you are not half a person. No person is ever going to complete you. They can complement you, but they can't be everything for you. At some point you have to do the hard work of loving yourself, making yourself happy, and becoming the partner you deserve.

CHAPTER 11

"No" Means Stop Asking

I ran for class president in high school and lost by one vote. The next year I was eligible to run for student body president. I ran again with a better campaign focused on the issues. I practiced my speech for weeks leading up to the election and delivered it flawlessly in front of the entire student body. My opponent showed up in jeans, without a prepared speech, and said that they wanted to have a fun year, then played a song they'd been working on. They won. I never ran opposed for another student leadership position.

At the women's college I attended, there are secret societies. These are kind of like sororities, except they each have a theme (singing, theater, humor, popularity). You aren't allowed to say you want to join, or you will be blacklisted. I screwed up and mentioned that I wanted to be in the club for academic excellence—off the record, of course. Selection night came. I could hear them singing in my hall and in the courtyard. They sang right past my door and never knocked. I stood there for an extra hour, their songs fading into the night, before I lost hope and went back to my homework. All of my other studious friends got in. I had exceptional grades, even better than some of the people they did pick. Didn't matter. I did not make the cut. A result I'd literally asked for.

I had a crush on this boy in college who had the most beautiful eyes you have ever seen. He was smart, cultured, and devilishly handsome. We had been flirty friends for months and I exclusively visited his fraternity house on my weekend escapades. One night we were hanging out in a room and everyone else decided to leave us alone. It was the first time we'd ever been by ourselves, and we looked at each other with "what now?" expressions. I finished my beer and tried to make a move. He shot it down—hard. It wouldn't have been so bad if he hadn't told the entire house I tried to pounce him. I got laughed out and never went back.

I have asked for a raise twice, ever, in my life. Both times my boss got offended by the ask and demanded to know why I thought I was better than what they were paying me. In both cases I'd prepared a compelling case for how I went above and beyond. I even calculated the number of dollars and hours that were being saved because of my initiative and improvements. In one case I'd saved the company almost a million dollars. In the other I'd found improvements that allowed for 33 percent more work to be done by the entire department without any new employees—saving at least one salary. My arguments were dismissed and I was told to sit down, shut up, and be grateful for my employment. For the record, I always went into these meetings nervous and humble and left feeling like the hairball my cat left for me overnight.

I stopped asking for things. I stopped taking initiative. It seemed like every time I went for something, I was met with humiliation. I heard the message loud and clear. Just accept what you have and be quiet.

The lie: "No" means stop asking.

* * *

How I squashed the lie:

I'm not very good at accepting what I have and being quiet. I would dream of a better life and have no idea how I was going to get it. I would attend conferences where people jumped around on stage and told me that "failure is not fatal." I would read self-help books that told stories of people who laughed in the face of rejection. Here are some examples:

1. **Thomas Edison** was told by his teachers that he was "too stupid to learn anything." Became one of the most famous and prolific inventors of all time, holding over one thousand patents.[31]

2. **Walt Disney** was fired from a newspaper because he "lacked imagination and had no good ideas."[32] Raise your hand if you've never seen a Disney movie. That's what I thought.

3. **Albert Einstein** couldn't speak until he was four. Thought to be mentally handicapped.[33] Failed his entrance exams to a Swiss Federal Polytechnic school.[34] Currently considered one

of the most brilliant minds of all time. Winner of a Nobel Prize in physics.[35]

4. **J.K. Rowling** started her writing career as a single mother on welfare.[36] Was turned down by twelve publishers for *Harry Potter,* which went on to sell over five hundred million copies.[37]

5. **Abraham Lincoln** failed in business multiple times. Failed at politics repeatedly. Went into war as a captain and left as a private—huge demotion.[38] Became America's sixteenth president and ended slavery in the US.[39]

6. **Oprah Winfrey** was fired from her first job as a TV anchor because she was "unfit for television."[40] Went on to create a media empire and became the first black female billionaire.[41]

7. **Michael Jordan** was cut from his high school basketball team.[42] Arguably the greatest player of all time.

8. **Jay-Z** was turned away by dozens of record labels. Since no one would sign him, he launched his record label and released his debut album himself. Has sold over thirty-six million albums and created Roc Nation (entertainment company) and Roc Nation Sports.[43]

9. **Colonel Sanders** tried and failed to sell his fried chicken franchise to over one thousand restaurants.[44] Today, there are over twenty-four thousand KFCs in 145 countries.[45]

10. **Harrison Ford** was told by the head of talent on his first movie, "You're never going to make it in the business, just forget about it."[46] Has made more than fifty movies[47] and is a cultural icon for the *Star Wars* and *Indiana Jones* franchises.

It's always inspiring to see what other people had to overcome on their way to success, but I never knew how to apply this until I took a negotiation class in grad school.

Negotiation is an alien concept to most Americans. Our culture teaches us to pay whatever is asked, without question. You don't go into the grocery store and start haggling with the clerk over the price of eggs. You just pay them.

When I thought about negotiating, the image of car dealerships and sleazy salespeople came to mind, and my palms started to sweat. I knew I needed to take this class because of how uncomfortable asking made me. I learned about ZOPAs (zone of possible agreement) and walkaway prices (the point at which you turn down the deal and leave). I learned how to always ask for more than I wanted, because I didn't know what the other person's limits were and if I started where I wanted to end up I'd miss every time.

I went through several mock negotiations with classmates and learned about different styles of negotiating and when each one was most effective. But what really helped was a trading exercise I had to do with a red paper clip.

If you don't know the inspiration behind this exercise, I'll summarize for you. Kyle MacDonald had a red paper clip and traded it for a fish pen. He traded that for a hand-carved doorknob. Which he traded for a Coleman camp stove with fuel. He continued trading up, and within one year and fourteen trades, he ended up with a two-story farmhouse in Canada.[48]

In class we were given a red paper clip and instructed to make at least five trades over six weeks. We were not allowed to tell anyone we were doing this for class or add to the trades. It had to be item for item. I traded my paper clip for a staple remover. I traded that for a box of staples. And that for a box of tea. And that for a box fan (lots of boxes). Finally I traded the box fan for a coffee table. My single paper clip got me a coffee table worth over a hundred dollars.

The key to the assignment was to ask for something I wanted in exchange for what I had. The trades went better when I asked for something specific instead of asking, "What will you give me for ___?"

I was uncomfortable the entire time, but I did end up having a lot of fun. I also learned that asking for something doesn't always mean rejection and that the worst that can happen is nothing.

* * *

How you can squash it too:

We have this fear of the negative feedback that might come with asking or trying. But 99.9 percent of the time, nothing horrific happens when you are told no. Your feelings might be a little hurt, but things don't get worse for you. For example: You apply for a new job. You don't even get an interview; they send you one of those form emails stating, "At this time we are moving forward with another candidate. We will keep your resume on file for other positions … blah blah blah."

Rejection. It sucks, but nothing actually changed. You didn't have a job when you woke up that morning and you still don't have it. Your life is in no way worse than before. All you did was create the potential to improve your situation.

That's all asking is, giving yourself the opportunity to have something better. If the worst that can happen is things stay the same, we should start asking for everything. I mean EVERYTHING.

Bible teacher and author Joyce Meyer said it best: "I would rather ask for a lot and get part of it than ask for a little and get all of it."[49]

Rejection can be less painful if you look at it appropriately. It can mean one of two things:

1. Not right now
2. It's not for me

Both of these are valid responses to your request and should be respected. However, they don't have to be the final result.

If you got a "not right now" type of no, figure out if you can change something to make it a yes. Is it something you can control or something that has to change for the other person? For example: You found a dream home and you've managed to scrape enough money together for a down payment. You get preapproved for a loan. You tour the home and make an early offer. The homeowner knows that it's a competitive market and holds out for other offers. You are asked for your best and highest offer by noon the following Monday. Then your agent calls to tell you that you were outbid. You lost the house. I understand how heartbreaking this scenario is, but it doesn't mean you can't ever have this house. It means you can't have it *right now*. Your choices are to wait for the house to come back on the market or find a new house. Either way the loss isn't permanent.

What about "it's not for me" types of nos? Easy—just say "next." Salespeople are familiar with this concept. Let's say you've discovered a way to have floors clean themselves. We can all agree that if you never had to sweep, vacuum, or mop again it would improve your life. Even so, there will be people who don't want that product. Maybe they secretly love pushing a vacuum around, maybe they like the smell of their floor cleaner, maybe they just don't want to pay for your solution. Doesn't matter. It's not for them. Your business, product, opinions, preferences, creativity … these things will never be for everyone. That's not a slight, it's just the way it is. Instead of allowing rejection to crush you, just move on to someone else. I realize I'm not everyone's cup of tea, but not everyone has good taste.

The difference between a setback and defeat is what you choose to accept. You will likely still be disappointed by a rejection, but you don't have to let it knock you out.

Here's a list of things you should start asking for immediately:

- **Help**. You don't have to be a martyr and do everything yourself. Ask for help.
- **An exception**. If things aren't as you like them, order off the menu. Ask for an exception to be made. Ask to partner with them to develop something new.
- **What you want**. You are allowed to have things the way you want them. Most of the time, we settle for less because we don't want to inconvenience anyone else. That's silly. What would make the situation better? Ask for that. It's no trouble to get things right.
- **Feedback**. Ask what you can do to improve. This one is hard because it's natural to fear the answer. But again, what's the worst that can happen? You can get better.
- **Favors**. Ask for and expect favors. Someone will get the big client, the best parking spot, an invitation to the Grammys. Why shouldn't it be you?

The key is you have to actually ask for those things. You can't hint at them. People don't read minds. Articulate what you would like and expect to be accommodated. It's uncomfortable at first, but I promise it gets better. More often than not when I ask for something I get it. It never ceases to surprise or elate me. I got so excited the other day because I ordered a chocolate *and* cookies-and-cream milkshake at Chick-fil-A. It's not a menu item, but they said it would be their pleasure to fill this request. It's delicious, if you're wondering.

If you never ask, the answer is always no. If you ask and the answer is no, then nothing changes. Start asking for everything and see what you can get.

P.S. Please tell me what you get. I love these stories. You can send me a note on my website www.nikkisoulsby.com or @ me on social media. Instagram: @nikki.soulsby. Twitter: @Nsoulsby. Facebook: nikkisoulsbyauthor.

CHAPTER 12

I Did It All Myself

I am a sucker for a good success story. Tell me how you hit rock bottom and dragged yourself back into the light. Tell me how everyone abandoned you and you succeeded anyway. Tell me how you lost all of your resources and rebuilt from nothing. I'm so here for it, and I'm not the only one. Society idealizes these kinds of stories. "It's the American dream, working your way up from nothing, armed with only your wits and a strong work ethic," says entrepreneur Jason Ford.[50]

I wanted the American dream. I wanted the big house and the SUV with the two kids and the husband who wore suits to work and mowed the lawn on weekends. I wanted to make it to the top based on my own efforts. I wanted to radiate success when I got there and be met with questions like "How did you do it?" and "What is your secret?" And I wanted to be able to dole out wisdom for those on the journey. In this fantasy I could tell them how I dragged myself out from the abyss and clawed my way to the top.

It was a hard journey, I sacrificed, but I made it, and the view was gorgeous. In this vision I was the only one at the top of my Everest.

I got a beautiful home, a car that I paid off, and a cat. I didn't need a husband going to work because I was a self-sufficient woman. I wore suits to the office. My life started improving after the dumpster fire that was 2017, and I was proud. I'd made it through the valley and was well on my way to that top I dreamed about.

I crawled up on my high horse and did a damn good job of feelin' myself. The view from the saddle showed all of the heartbreak and failure I'd overcome and the tireless, endless hours of effort. I knew that each time a valley came, I would find my own way back into the light. No one handed me jack—ever. I took 100 percent responsibility and 100 percent credit for my outcomes.

The lie: **I did it all myself.**

***

How I squashed the lie:

On one of my high-horse days, I called my mom. Now, my mom is a no-nonsense redhead who you do not want to mess with. I get all of my sharp wit from her, and she's been sharper and wittier longer than I have, so she's better at it. We talk regularly about this and that, but on this specific call I was regaling her with all of my accomplishments. I started droning on about how I made it in spite of everything, how I was living my best life, and how it was extra impressive because no one helped me. I was 100 percent self-made.

My mom was having none of this baloney. "Nikki, you are not self-made."

"I beg your pardon?"

"You have a house because you have a decent job, which you wouldn't have without your degree. A degree your stepdad and I helped pay for … "

"Okay, I did have a little financial help, but I did the work to get my scholarship. I'm the one who gave my entire savings to pay tuition. I'm the one who pulled forty-hour workweeks on top of a full class load and still graduated magna cum laude. No one did any of that for me. No one helped me get any of my internships. Absolutely no one has ever helped me get a job. I had to fight to get a foot in the door. I've never been fast-tracked at work. The only time I even got promoted was when one of my coworkers reported the open misogyny in the office and the company found out she had a case. Then I got a promotion because I was a woman. No one has ever recognized my effort, even though I did more than twice as much as anyone else. I had to scrap my way into better positions. I did that—me. So if I have nice things, it's because I worked my ass off for them and saved! Why can't you just be proud of me?"

"I am proud of you. Of course I'm proud of you, but I'm trying to get you to understand and appreciate that you did not get where you are by yourself. Just think about it."

So I did. I thought about it.

Y'all, I hate being wrong. In this instance I wasn't just a little wrong—I was big-time wrong. I had so many privileges and then I had the audacity to claim my victories as solo achievements, without acknowledging everyone and everything that helped me behind the scenes.

Privilege 1: I have never really had to struggle for anything. I've always been fed, sheltered, and loved. There were times when money was tight, or I was unemployed and wondering how I was going to make rent, but I never starved and I was never evicted.

Privilege 2: I have only ever attended private schools. Private schools are known for their high-quality education, but the biggest advantage here is the environment. With smaller class sizes, you get more attention. Also, your classmates are equally privileged. It creates a cycle of success and good choices. For example, the worst influences I ever had were a couple of my friends in high school who smoked a little weed on the weekends and watched R-rated movies.

Privilege 3: I don't have student loans. In undergrad that came from a combination of scholarship money, my own contributions, and some help from my parents. In grad school I did take out some loans, but paid them off before I even graduated by selling my house and downsizing to an apartment.

Privilege 4: I'm white. I'm not even remotely ethnically ambiguous. I'm the kind of white it hurts to look at in the sun. I have gotten sunburned driving across town in my car (hand to God).

Privilege 5: I'm Christian. I don't have to take PTO for major religious holidays, because they are usually covered. I don't have to hide my faith in order to overcome ignorant bias.

Privilege 6: I pass as a cisgender heterosexual. While I am cisgender, I'm not strictly heterosexual. I love people for who they are; it doesn't have anything to do with gender. I've had loving, wonderful relationships with both women and men. But because I married a heterosexual man, I don't face any discrimination.

Privilege 7: I'm abnormally good at reading. When I took my college entrance exams, I got a perfect score in the reading section (with time left over). I read fast, pick up concepts easily, and remember what I learned. Because reading is easy, I do it a lot. I read about a hundred books a year in my free time, which gives me a distinct advantage over people who struggle with learning. I can't stress enough the advantage this brings.

"Having privilege means having an advantage that is outside of your control and that you didn't ask for," according to Hive Learning's "5 Main Types of Privilege."[51] If I made a list of all of the forms of privilege, I think I would check every box except being male. I have a *lot* of privilege.

Those privileges allowed me to do things like attend the college of my choice. The freedom to work and support only myself and not my parents or siblings. Knowledge about how to manage my finances wisely and how to plan for my future. The confidence to apply for any job at any company that I was remotely qualified for and trust that my application would be given full consideration. The gall to apply to a top 10 MBA program after showing little to no professional accomplishments.

I am undeniably advantaged, but I am also undeniably blessed by a preponderance of great people in my life. My parents worked hard to not only provide for my physical and emotional needs but also to coach me through tough choices and new experiences. When I wanted to buy my first house, I called my mom and asked her what on earth I needed to do. My educators cared about my learning and also took the time to become experts and learn how to teach. I'm so thankful for their work. Oh sure, I've had my share of bad bosses and really awful mentors, but I have also had more than my fair share of good working conditions and outstanding colleagues, mentors, and leaders. My husband puts up with all of my bullshit and loves me through it. My friends, coworkers, family, husband, fellow volunteers, teachers, mentors, and coaches have all had a hand in making me better.

There is no doubt I've gotten through hard times. I've survived situations that I hope no one else has to ever live through. I have made good decisions and bad decisions, and I learned from both. I still take responsibility for my attitude and my actions. But I would be completely out of line to say that I accomplished a single thing by myself. I have been blessed by the excellence, effort, and enduring love of thousands of other people. And I am just so grateful.

* * *

How you can squash it too:

In my econ classes, we learned that no man is an island. Every person who has loved, encouraged, inspired, taught, helped, served, influenced, or mentored you is partially responsible for any ounce of your success. You definitely have to do the work, but you never do it alone.

When someone does something impressive, the first question we ask is, How did you do it? We assume *they* are the secret. They probably have some solid advice for how to do whatever they've done, but they themselves are also a product of the work of others.

The whole point of this book is to inspire you to take control of your thoughts and improve your life. All of my messages end with things you, personally, can do to make your life better. But I want you to know that you do not exist in a vacuum. You can succeed, but you will never do it by yourself.

Let's say you're a painter who makes a million dollars a year selling your work. No one can make your art but you. However, someone else made the paint and the canvas. Someone built the area you work in. People are working so that you can have water, electricity, internet service, and food. In order to make a million dollars a year, you have to sell your work. How do people find your work? Is there a gallery that shows it? Do you post it on a website or on social media? What about your customers? If you discount everything else, you have to admit that other people's money is 100 percent responsible for making you a "self-made" millionaire. You get the point. Other people are important.

You do get to be captain of your own life and choose what you want to do and where you want to go, but you can't do it all alone. Accepting this is not weakness, it's a strength. Since you no longer have to have the answer to every problem, you can focus on having the answer to the problems you are best suited to fix. While you're out there crushing it, setting new records, and achieving the unbelievable, take a few moments to be grateful to everyone and everything that enables you to do this.

Here are some of my favorite ways to show appreciation:

1. **Tell people you appreciate them and use relevant examples.** Saying "I appreciate how you always make me feel important. It means a lot to me" is way better than "I appreciate you."

2. **Do something small but thoughtful for them,** like emptying the dishwasher or bringing them coffee.

3. **Give good hugs!** If you're not a hugger or they aren't a hugger, give them a solid handshake or a genuine smile.

4. **Give people your full attention.** Put down the phone for five minutes and really listen when they are talking to you.

5. **Be an encourager.** Remind them of how capable they are and how much you believe in them. Praise is like money—you can never have too much of it.

6. **Surprise them with something they love or have always wanted to try.** One of my coworkers once drove me to the airport. This should have been an easy trip, but we got stuck in awful traffic for three hours *and* someone rear-ended her car (he fell asleep at the wheel). I sent her flowers as a thank you, and she called me crying when she got them. Totally worth it.

7. **Devote an evening to celebrating them.** I took my husband on a date. We went to his favorite restaurant, got his favorite dessert, and talked about his accomplishments. He does a great job making me feel loved and special, so I figured it was my turn to return the kindness.

8. **Give compliments.** This is my favorite free thing to give away. Whether you know someone well or not, a genuine compliment makes you both feel better. This goes over well with the invisible people of our society. The administrative assistants, parking attendants, and janitors of the world. Just because their work is quiet doesn't mean we shouldn't acknowledge it.

9. **Tip!** I worked in restaurant service for years. I don't care how nice you were to me, how good you thought the meal was, or if you told me I did a great job. If your tip doesn't reflect the level of service I gave you, I'm insulted.

10. **Smile.** Wearing your mean mug won't make anyone feel any better. Smiles are for everyone, even strangers.

11. **Brag about them to their manager.** Not only do you show appreciation for the person, you could help their career.

12. **Write a note and stick it where they can find it.** You can sign it or leave it anonymous. Up to you.

13. **Blast them with positive thoughts.** It sounds weird, but I read about someone who went around giving "love bombs" to people.[52] They would focus their positive energy on a person and blast them with love and good feelings. They even did this to strangers in traffic! It's so fun. You should try it.

14. **Offer to help.** If you can make their life easier, even for a few minutes, just do it.

15. **Donuts.** You can't go wrong by bringing donuts.

Showing gratitude is a way to improve your energy. You not only brighten someone else's day but you usually brighten your own as well. This also sets up support in your future. When you show appreciation, people want to go out of their way to help you, because they know you'll notice.

No matter how independent you are, you are *not* self-made. Sorry, Charlie. You are a product of the people in your life. This is nothing to be ashamed of. Rather, it's something to be incredibly grateful for. Create positive energy for yourself and the people in your life by practicing active appreciation.

CHAPTER 13

I Can't Control My Feelings

Trigger warning for self-harm.
Please skip if you are uncomfortable with this material.

YOU know when your life turns into the perfect storm? When it feels like you're being attacked on all sides and you are wondering when something will let up? This happened to me when I was sixteen.

My parents started a divorce when I was thirteen. Divorce is hard for everyone, but it's especially hard when it turns ugly. My parents used to fight a lot. So when they told me they were divorcing, I was relieved. I thought maybe I wouldn't have to sing over their screaming anymore. Not so much. The divorce dragged on for years. I think most children want to maintain relationships with both of their parents through a divorce, and I wasn't any different. I tried to see both sides. I tried to make peace. I tried to protect my siblings and minimize the talk about the other parent. It didn't work.

By the time I was sixteen, my dad got remarried to a woman who did not like me. Usually this wasn't a problem because I lived with my mom full time. But weekends at my dad's house were very stressful. I was held to ridiculous standards and always seemed to come up short. I remember one time I went to a birthday party at a friend's house. I say "party" loosely, because at a Christian school, party just means twenty to thirty kids eating pizza and watching the newest blockbuster release. A friend asked for a ride home, and I called my dad and stepmom to ask if it was okay. It would make me about five minutes late for curfew. I got the go-ahead and dropped my friend off. Small problem: I had underestimated the time and was eight minutes late. This, apparently, was unacceptable. My stepmom flew into a rage, yelled at me for being spoiled and irresponsible, and took my car away for a month.

I was sad to lose my car but really stressed because I was supposed to take my siblings to school. I dreaded having to tell my mom that she would have to drive us for a whole month. She took it better than I thought, but I still felt like a disappointment. My wings had been clipped.

The next week I found out that my best friend had slept with my boyfriend. They were now an item and were not speaking to me. I didn't understand. I had no one to talk to about what was going on, I got dumped, and now I had to watch the two of them make out in the hallway between every class.

I told you my parents' divorce was nasty, but in the same week it got worse. They went from custody battles to lawsuits. I would love to tell you all the gory details, but for the sake of not getting sued myself let's just say my dad's behavior was less than honorable. I was never sure which father I was going to get when it came time to visit. Sometimes he seemed to genuinely miss having me around. Other times he pumped me for information about my mother. The worst was when he tried crying at me. He would give a weepy monologue about how much he loved me, but it was always laced with guilt about how I didn't love him enough. When your dad cries, it's really uncomfortable, especially when you're sixteen. If I didn't give him the reaction he wanted, the tears would stop and he'd snap into an angry fit. He would scream at me for being disrespectful, not living up to his expectations, and, basically, being the absolute worst.

Home was bad. School was bad. My best friend was gone. My heart was broken. My stepmom had taken my one freedom. Oh, and I got grounded because I tanked a test at school. I started throwing up every day because the sheer awfulness was too much for my body. My insides went from feeling tight to shaky to painful to absolutely numb. I had nothing left.

I didn't know what to do. I was drowning in a confusing sea of emotion and there was no way out. So I popped ten ibuprofen and put a nasty slash down my wrist with a steak knife.

I wasn't trying to die, I was trying to feel.

Let me be VERY clear here. This was not an appropriate response for my feelings. This was not healthy or rational behavior. I do not encourage self-harm in any way. I was hormonal, immature, and dealing with some heavy shit. I tried to find an easy way to make it stop. It didn't work—at all. My mom was furious. I got suspended from school. I was sent to therapy. I was grounded (again) for a long time.

The lie: I can't control my feelings.

***

How I squashed the lie:

It took four more years for me to learn a truth that changed my life: I am 100 percent in control of my attitude and actions.

My review of network marketing businesses hasn't been glowing up to this point, but I have to give credit where it's due. I learned a lot about self-help, success principles, and the entrepreneurial mindset from that experience. I have been to sixty-plus conferences; read over two hundred books on business, leadership, and self-help; and had one-on-one coaching sessions with some of the most successful businesspeople in North Carolina. They all told me at one point or another that my actions and attitude were my choice.

I know what you're thinking—bad shit happens, and it's not your fault. You are absolutely right. It's so easy to point to circumstances and other people as the source of your problems. I won't even argue that these things don't have a major influence on your life. But they don't get to decide your attitude or actions. That's all you, baby.

I wish I'd had the tools at sixteen to handle all of that negative shit life was throwing at me. I wish I'd known that I had other options and that other people didn't get to ruin my life. I wasn't equipped and I responded poorly. I probably made the situation worse by spiraling.

But the next time the storms came for me, I had another option. I can't say I applied the principle well, but I did apply it and it helped. The next time my life went sideways was when I was sexually assaulted. As someone who was previously suicidal, this could have been a huge trigger for me, but by then I could control my reactions (sort of). So instead of checking out when the worst happened, I went into hiding. I wasn't ready to reframe or manage all of my responses. For several weeks I minimized my exposure to anything and tried to recover. Eventually my attitude improved enough for me to choose better things. It still took years to recover, but it was a huge win that I didn't turn to suicide as the answer or allow the situation to permanently stunt my life. Bad stuff happened, but the bad stuff didn't own me.

This is not a message on positive thinking and speaking "as if." No, you are entitled to feel every feeling that comes into your body. Not only that, but you should feel them completely. You should embrace every horrible, gut-wrenching, headache-inducing feeling. Then you should sit down and decide what you want to do. Are you going to let them eat you alive or let them pass?

Sometimes you need to let the feeling sit for a while before you're ready to let it go. That's okay. You can sit with something as long as you need to. I like to give myself a deadline for my feelings. When bad things happen and I start to feel some kind of way, I give myself a day or three to wallow in emotions and self-pity. Then I pick a time that I will stop allowing it to dominate me. For example, I'm allowed to steep in my feelings and feel sorry for myself until 5 p.m. tomorrow. Then I'm going to take this shithole and make something awesome out of it. But I'm not doing that until then. I'll do whatever I need to experience my response to what just happened, but I will not let it break me.

By taking control of my attitude and actions, I got better at responding to the bad stuff. I took the things that tried to kill me and used them to make my life bigger. I took my heartbreaks and turned them into empathy. I took unreasonably cruel situations and turned them into kindness. Situations and people have tried to break me, but I'm a diamond, darling, I don't crack.

* * *

How you can squash it too:

Feelings are temporary. No matter what is crushing your soul today, it will pass. Good feelings pass too. You won't always feel inspired and motivated. You won't always be proud of yourself. You won't always be happy. But you can always choose to focus on the positive and decide to respond to every situation in a way that best serves you and your goals.

Emotions may start spontaneously, but they grow stronger the more you let them show up. Maybe you trip in public and thud loudly in front of strangers. The immediate emotion you feel will be embarrassment. If you keep thinking about the situation and focusing on the embarrassment, it will get bigger. Bigger, in this case, doesn't mean better—it means harder to get rid of. Allowing emotions to hang around is like pouring water on a mogwai— gremlins show up and try to ruin everything.

To move past an emotion you must first acknowledge it. Then you have to examine it and decide if it's helpful or harmful. If it's helpful keep it, but if it's harmful reframe it. Reframing means just looking at something from a different perspective. Unless you're a naturally positive person, you might have to try several perspectives to find one that's going to serve you. But if you look hard enough, you can find the good in anything. Once you have a new perspective, it gets infinitely easier to let a bad emotion go. If an emotion tries to come back, just treat it like an annoying coworker—give a head nod, and find anything else to do.

Growing emotions by focusing on them works in the positive too. It's easy for us to recall a time when we felt embarrassed, sad, or angry, but it's just as easy to recall a time when we felt passionate, excited, or at peace. Emotions grow to accommodate the space you give them. In order to experience more positive emotions, you have to purposefully make them repeat in your head. It might take a little more effort in the beginning, but as positive emotions get bigger and stronger, your thought patterns will start to shift to these kinds of thoughts. You'll start looking for the good or feeling happy when nothing is going on.

Thibaut Meurisse, author of *Master Your Emotions*, says there are two ways for you to manage your emotions:

1. You can use your posture, vocal inflection, or even eye position to influence how you feel. If you stand with your shoulders slumped and eyes down and talk slowly, you are more likely to feel depressed. If you stand straight up, roll your shoulders back, put your hands on your hips, and look up, it will be hard for you to feel anything but confident. If you talk excitedly, you'll start to feel excited. If you talk like you're bored, you will feel bored.

2. You can manage your environment. Begin to notice situations where you feel good and, alternatively, where you feel bad. Try to do more things that make you feel good and less that bring up negative emotions. An easy target here is social media. If scrolling Instagram makes you feel connected to your friends and leaves you laughing at the newest Reel, by all means keep scrolling. But if

Kylie Jenner's newest swimsuit pic is going to make you feel self-conscious or if the documentation of everyone else's exotic trips is making you feel inferior, PUT THE PHONE DOWN. Do something else.

You can't control when emotions happen or which emotions show up, but you can manage how much room you give them and how you respond to them. Tony Robbins has a funny way of changing your response to negative emotions called "interrupting."[53] When the emotion shows up and you aren't ready for a reframe, just interrupt yourself by doing something ridiculous. When you start rehashing that fight with your mom again, stop yourself mid-thought and say out loud, "OOGA BOOGA!" Every time the fight starts to creep in, stop it with the "OOGA BOOGA!" Eventually you won't be able to think about the fight without laughing because it's so stupid to shout "OOGA BOOGA!" over and over.

Bad things will happen. You don't have a choice. Situations will turn sour, people will let you down, you might let yourself down, or you might just have a rotten day. You can't control any of that. You can control how you respond and how you let something affect your attitude. You are stronger than you give yourself credit for. I promise. By controlling your emotions, you can control your attitude. By controlling your attitude, you can more easily choose better actions. Once you've got these things locked in, you can control your destiny. You can process any situation in a healthy way *and* respond to it in a way that works for you and your dreams. You are the boss of your attitude and your actions.

The next time the storm comes for you, you'll be ready. Instead of it railroading you into oblivion, you'll be able to look it dead in the face, put both middle fingers up, and sashay through it.

CHAPTER 14

The Little Things Don't Matter

I'M allergic to running.

No joke, my body rejects running unless I've trained it to accept that this is what we are doing. I can make it approximately 0.65 miles before my skin starts to crawl. I develop an uncontrollable itch that gets worse if I scratch it and drives me mad if I don't. On more than one occasion, I have drawn blood from intense scratching. The itch only happens in my jiggly bits. You know, my bingo arms, my love handles, my thighs, my tush … all the places you want to be scratching in public.

I can get past the itch, but it takes about two weeks of running three times a week. As long as I keep running at least twice a week, the itching stays at bay and I can get on with my life. This doesn't set me up to be the next Usain Bolt, but it does give me an excuse to not do that kind of cardio.

For some reason I got it in my head that I was going to run a half-marathon. At the time the only part of me that ran was my mouth. At the end of the year when I was setting goals, I decided a half-marathon was the ticket. So I registered for a race twenty weeks out.

Surely I could get into half-marathon shape in twenty weeks. I didn't mean to win the thing, I just wanted to finish. So I did an online search for half-marathon training plans and got to work. I had a training schedule and stuck to it religiously. I ran five days a week, no matter the weather and no matter what else I had on my schedule. I was committed.

That first run was hard. Not only did I have to fight the itch, but I had to fight the rest of my body as well. My legs did not appreciate their new task, and my lungs burned most of the time. I had to take five or six walk breaks in the twenty-five minutes it took me to do a single mile.

After the requisite two weeks, the itching went away, but I still had to fight soreness for at least a month. It was not fun. When I got through the worst of it, I could run a couple of miles without stopping. I was so stinking proud. I had never run more than two consecutive miles!

I read articles and books on running, and they recommended all sorts of things that could help my running, like stretching before and after a run, cleaning up my diet, and cross-training. I stretched sometimes, but the rest I ignored. I wanted to run, not swim or bike—how would adding those exercises into an already-grueling training program help? I'd just wear myself out.

I did improve, though. My long runs got longer, but so did my short runs. I remember how wild it felt to have a five-mile short run. I almost didn't believe I could do it, but I did. You should have seen me strut out of the gym that day. For the record, I did my short runs on a treadmill and long runs outside.

I prepared hard for nineteen weeks straight ... and then I blew out my knee four days before the event. Cue devastation. I'd spent good money to run this race and now I was injured, losing money, and failing at my goal. I'm not sure which emotion dominated, but it was a solid mix of anger, frustration, sadness, and pain.

I didn't understand what went wrong. I ran five days a week and increased my distance appropriately (no more than 10 percent per week). There was no reason I should be injured. And yet ...

The lie: **the little things don't matter.**

---

* * *

How I squashed the lie:

The frustration from my first race put me off running for a couple of years. I still went to the gym, but I focused on things like the elliptical machine or weight lifting. Then a friend at work inspired me to try again. She trained for and ran a half-marathon in twelve weeks. I figured if she could do it, I could do it.

I couldn't have a repeat of my last half-marathon performance. So I started researching what the best distance runners do. I found not just a running schedule but a whole training program put together by people who were ultramarathoners. If anyone knew how to run without injury, it had to be these people. I was ready for their program to kick my butt into gear and have me running seven days a week, but that didn't happen. I still had a four-day running schedule, but I had cross-training twice a week, weight lifting a couple of times, stretching daily, and at least one foam rolling session. I had no idea what foam rolling was but I figured it out (thanks, YouTube). They also required at least two complete rest days, which meant I had to double up on my workouts other days. Sometimes this meant getting up early and working out before work (*groan*).

Once I got through that awful two weeks when the itch tried to kill me, I made it to a place where I could focus on the work. I got obsessed. Y'all know it was serious when I started eating salad on purpose. Salad and I are not friends. It's not salad's fault; it's mine. My taste buds work too well, and I can't convince my brain that watery fiber is ever a superior meal choice.

The most amazing thing started happening. Even though my runs were getting longer, they started feeling easier. My energy levels picked up. My attitude improved. My confidence was soaring. This time when I hit my ten-mile-long run I didn't look (or feel) like roadkill afterward. I felt powerful.

I ran 13.1 miles in two hours, twenty-five minutes, and twenty-seven seconds, beating my goal time of two hours, thirty minutes! The sense of achievement that comes from working your ass off and winning is indescribable. It's relief mixed with excitement mixed with confidence. Clearly, I was an athlete ... kind of. So why didn't my first training program work?

I didn't do the little things.

It is no shock to learn that you have to run a lot to train for a half-marathon, but that's not everything you need to get to the goal. I was asking a lot of my body and not giving it anything in return. I was demanding more, more, more, and showing it zero respect in the process. Of course it gave out on me. It was unfortunate that it happened right before my race, but it wasn't surprising. Stretching, foam rolling, resting, cross-training, and eating to support running are all easy to skip. They are little things, but these little things make a huge difference in the quality of training and the end result. When I consistently added the little things, my runs were faster, hills got easier, and I had way more energy. Doing those little things supercharged my running efforts.

Not in the beginning, though. In the beginning it was annoying to stretch so much. I didn't like foam rolling, I hated eating clean, and I wanted to stay up late watching Netflix. But I kept doing the little things and eventually started seeing results. Then I started seeing big results. By the end, I had taken over five minutes off my mile time. Don't be too impressed, I'm still slow, but it was massive progress. Also, I looked really good. I wasn't running to lose weight, but my body sculpted itself into a thing of beauty by the end. I had the waist I'd always dreamed about. The best part was that I looked forward to running. It wasn't a chore to do, it was a pleasure. Because I didn't hurt and had extra energy, it was fun to get out there and move.

The thing about getting results is that you can't just focus on parts of the process and hope to get there. You have to pay the full price. It's like walking up to a vending machine that charges one dollar for a soft drink, sticking in ninety cents, then getting mad at the machine for not spitting out a drink. You can't shortchange what success demands. My first race attempt was more like a sixty-cent contribution to something that costs one dollar. I did the most important thing, but I didn't do *everything* required to get where I wanted.

* * *

How you can squash it too:

Invisible actions are the hardest to appreciate. They are not sexy. No one sees them or knows whether or not you've done them. You can completely blow them off for a while and not even get into trouble. It only starts to matter when those little actions or inactions add up.

This is a pesky little law of success called the compound effect[54] or the slight edge,[55] depending on which book you read. The basic concept is that little actions (or inactions) multiply over time to create massive results.

Most people are familiar with the concept of compounding interest, which we talked about in chapter 5. A little bit of money today, invested with interest, will create a large amount of money later. Gobs more than what you ever personally contribute. The trick is to not get discouraged in the beginning when the earned interest is small. If you have $1,000 today and invest it at a tremendous 10 percent interest rate, you'd end up with $1,100 at the end of the year. That's not nothing, but you're not quitting your day job with an extra hundred bucks. If you were twenty-five when you invested this money and never added another dime, you'd more than double your initial investment in ten years. What?! Ten years to get another $1,000? That's slow! Yep, but if you leave that money in that same investment for forty years, you'd have $41,145. Not too bad for investing $1,000 forty years ago. If instead of the one-time contribution of $1,000 you did annual contributions of $1,000, your total contribution over forty years would be $40,000, and your final account balance would be $442,593!

The compound effect says that the little things will get you—the ones I call invisible actions. No one knows if you do them. No one knows if you miss a day. There are no immediate results, which is why they are so easy to skip.

I bet you're already a secret ninja at compounding and you don't even know it. I assume you brush your teeth every day (at least I hope so). I'm not talking about a perfect oral hygiene routine with the floss and the electric toothbrush and the mouthwash ... I mean you, toothbrush, some kind of toothpaste, and one to two minutes. Do you do it? Yep. Would anything happen if you skip tomorrow? Not really. You'd probably have some nasty breath, but your teeth would be fine. But if you skipped for the next six months, your dentist might have some concerns. If you just stopped forever, the actual tooth fairy would show up with their fluoride blaster and tackle you to the ground. Oh, and your teeth will have rotted out of your head.

Brushing your teeth takes moments. It's not hard. No one knows if you do it. There are no immediate consequences to skipping, but that's the thing. Immediate. There are definitely consequences for skipping all of your little daily activities eventually.

It's harder to skip the big activities. People notice. The consequences happen much faster. If I just stopped going into work, I might not get in trouble for one day. If I skipped for a whole week (just because), I'm pretty sure they'd either fire me or write me a personal development plan and file it with HR. I definitely couldn't pull that off twice.

But showing up to work is a big action. What about the little ones? What about leaving ten minutes early? If you're extra sneaky, no one will even know you do it ... at first. Eventually people will figure it out. It probably won't tank your career to skip those last ten minutes of the day, but it certainly won't help your case for any kind of career advancement. It's so insignificant it shouldn't count, but it does.

Eating one salad won't change your pant size. Believe me, I've tried, and y'all know how I feel about salad. Going to The Cheesecake Factory one time also won't change your pant size. Getting one new customer is probably not going to make a huge difference in your commission, but if you got one each week or each month you'd see tremendous growth. If you wrote one page a day, you'd finish a book. If you hugged people one to two seconds longer, you'd both feel better. Please don't be an over-hugger, though. That gets creepy.

So how do we use the law of compounding to our advantage?

1. **Awareness.** You have to be aware of the little things to know if they are working for you or not. This starts with knowing what you're already doing. You can do this by tracking your current habits: counting calories or going through your spending trends on Mint. Whatever you're working on, make a list of all of the things you are currently doing (or not doing) in that area.

2. **Analysis.** Now that you know what you are doing, analyze whether those things are working for or against you. You're probably not doing big things to take you off track, but there may be some little things that aren't helping you. Some of the bad habits I have to cut back on (regularly) are Starbucks, Amazon, and Chick-fil-A. My wallet and my waistline do not appreciate the compound effect of money and time spent with these friends. Not all little actions are important ones, though, so don't get hung up on the details.

3. **Action.** Whatever is getting in your way is a small habit
    you've created. You have to keep awareness of this habit until
    you replace it with a better one. I find that continual tracking
    coupled with a weekly or monthly check-in helps me. When
    I started drinking more water, I'd make a check mark on my
    planner for days I drank the water. Just the accountability of
    this check mark often helped reinforce this new habit. At the
    end of the week, I could see how my habit was doing. At the
    end of the month, I could see solid improvement. Eventually,
    drinking more water became the norm. It was a little action
    working in my favor, and I didn't have to stress over it.

If you can believe that the snooze button gives you more rest,
then you can believe in the concept of compounding interest. I
want you to make little investments in yourself and your dreams
on a consistent basis and watch what happens. You don't have to
revamp your whole life, just make a tiny change. Read ten pages of
a book each day. Spend one hour working on your side hustle. Cut
out one cup of coffee. Give yourself an extra thirty minutes on that
project for work. Add a single serving of fruit to one meal.

Compound interest is the eighth wonder of the world.
He who understands it, earns it. He who doesn't,
pays it. —Albert Einstein[56]

CHAPTER 15

I Just Need to Work Harder

A fitness guru once wrote that the secret to the sexy, sculpted body of my dreams was powerlifting plus insane amounts of protein. This was long before the days when I was happy with my body. I was reading everything I could to get an edge in my workouts or nutrition. This book made a compelling argument. So I went all in.

Powerlifting is a sport dedicated to lifting the most weight possible using certain maneuvers: bench press, squat, and deadlift. They focus on a one-rep max, which means the most weight you can move (properly) one time. It requires zero endurance and 100 percent power. Hence the name.

I have to admit something: the weight room at the gym makes me nervous. I know I have just as much of a right to be there as anyone else, but it still feels like I'm in someone else's way. It was especially hard in the beginning, because I would grab my little baby weights and go to work … right next to Mr. Universe. The guy would be doing bicep curls with my body weight and I would be struggling to get just the barbell up in a deadlift. I could talk about this "I don't deserve to be here mentality," but that's not the point of this chapter. I'm getting there.

I showed up four times a week with my notebook, a pen, and determination. I have to write stuff down or it flies out of my head. This includes what exercises I do, for how long or for how many reps, and at what pace or weight. It looks a little nerdy to carry a notebook and pen around the gym, but it helped. My runs got longer, my lifts got heavier, and—shock of all shocks—my muscles showed up. After that I only wore tank tops to the gym because I wanted to keep seeing the muscles grow.

Every couple of days, I saw this group of women come in, and take over a squat rack and a bench press for about an hour. They lifted HEAVY. By sheer luck I swapped my normal leg day for a powerlifting day and ended up working next to them. When you're the only four women in the power lifting section, it's not hard to make friends. They called themselves the Barbellas and worked out three times a week. This was not a cute little girls club. No, they commanded massive respect on the days they came in and threw around weights that would intimidate most men. It was such a treat to work with them. They corrected my form and pushed me harder than I ever pushed myself. On my best day, I did a 135-pound bench press, 200-pound squat, and 225-pound dead-lift. Go ahead, you can be impressed.

They weren't there every day, though, so I had to do some workouts without them. Not a problem, I was strong now. I had this shit. There were a couple of times when I almost got stuck in a lift, but I was always able to muscle my way through. Oorah!

Then something happened. It was a Wednesday (chest day), and I walked in to find an open bench. This was a miracle I wasn't going to pass up. I snagged it and started doing my warmup lifts. I crushed them. I did my heavier warmup lifts and crushed them too. It was going to be an awesome day. I thought I might even set a PR (personal record). So I skipped the last set of warmup lifts and threw fifty more pounds on my bar. I positioned my shoulders on the bench, planted my feet, and curled my hands around the metal. I got the weight up without any problem. I brought it down, slow and controlled, to my chest and started pushing it back up. That's when my left arm turned to Jell-O and stopped working.

I had my right arm almost high enough to rack the weight, but I couldn't get it over the lip. So I took a deep breath and tried to muscle it up. I dug deep. I pushed hard. And the bar started coming back down. No! I was trapped. I tried getting some momentum with a little rocking, but this just turned into being stuck in an awkward and kind of painful position. I had pinned myself under a hundred-plus-pound bar, and there was no way I could escape.

So I did what any self-respecting woman in the weight section would do if they were trapped by their own arrogance. I yelled, "Help!" The guy doing pull-ups in front of me dropped down, hurdled the bench between us, and came to my rescue. He grabbed the bar with both hands and racked it effortlessly. He even stayed to give me a hand up and make sure I was okay. Physically I was fine, but I'd bruised my ego pretty good. I turned seventeen shades of purple, thanked him for his help, and tried to sneak out without being noticed.

The lie: I just need to work harder.

***

How I squashed the lie:

About a year into working for my current company, a couple of situations came up that made things … challenging. We were a three-person department: me, my coworker, and my supervisor. We didn't have great numbers, but we were incredibly effective and worked well together. Then my coworker got an opportunity outside the company and left us. It was the best move for him, and he was smart to make it, but it meant that all of his work now had to be done by me and my boss until we found a replacement.

I absorbed most of this work and buckled down on my focus and productivity to make sure I wasn't dropping anything. If I was just more organized, I could fit everything in and still make it home to do my homework on time. Then the other shoe dropped—my boss also decided to leave the company.

I understood her need to leave and supported her position, but now things got really tricky. I had become a one-woman show doing the work of three people. I was in the middle of my MBA program and didn't have the luxury of working longer hours, but I had to stay employed and make sure I hit all of my former team's targets. I went to my clutch move when things went wrong—work harder.

I got up earlier and stayed as late as I could. I smooshed as much work into a ten-hour day as I could. I was laser-focused and delivering quality work to our superiors. But I was so tired. I could feel the constant pump of energy and adrenaline begin to take a toll on my mental and physical health. I got a cold and started getting migraines. Something had to give. Working harder was not cutting it anymore.

So I did some research and found a new way. I read a book called *Essentialism*[57] that changed my life. Greg McKeown taught me how to focus on what contributed the most value and let everything else go. I coupled this advice with wisdom from *The 4-Hour Workweek*.[58] Tim Ferriss makes a number of interesting points in that book, but the nugget I needed most at this moment was *automation*.

There was no way I could fit three full-time jobs into an eight-to-ten-hour day, go home and power through executive-level MBA homework, and still have a functioning brain. I had to create a better way. So I prioritized, automated, and used our virtual assistants to outsource what I could. I took every opportunity to understand the needs of each person requiring work from me, then I reworked how to deliver that without any extra crap and in the most efficient way possible.

In about six weeks I had turned my ten-hour days back into eight-hour days, and I even got to reinstate my lunch hour. I never missed a single deliverable, deadline, or request. In fact, I was so good at being a department of one that they let me do it for six months. Then they decided I needed a manager (palms up emoji). My pay band was too low to merit autonomy; even though I had proved for half a year that I could produce outstanding work without a supervisor, they hired one anyway. I swear to you, they hired someone to watch me work and paid him about $40,000 more than I was making to do it.

This only lasted for about four months before I got scooped up by another team who knew my work and realized they needed someone like me on their team.

I learned three things during this little period of trial and tribulation:

1. I am capable of *way* more than I ever thought possible.

2. I can't always just outwork the problem.

3. My first answer isn't always my best answer.

***

How you can squash it too:

When you're faced with a challenge, what is your go-to move? Do you find an easy answer and stick with it, or do you probe a little deeper and look for something better?

If you're like me, when stuff starts going wrong you feel like you need to double down and work harder. You feel like you can *make it happen* if you just try harder, believe harder, pray harder, sweat more, or get more disciplined. And sometimes that will work.

But what about when you're out of time, money, energy, or faith? What happens when you don't *have* anything more to throw at the task? What then?

That's when you find real solutions and not just easy fixes. Let me tell you a story. A property management company in New York City was getting a lot of complaints from their tenants about slow elevators. These weren't just suggestion box rants; people were genuinely upset about the elevator speed and threatening to break their leases and leave the building because of this gigantic inconvenience. Obviously the property management company started taking this seriously when the threat of vacant apartments came up. They pulled their leadership team together and asked what could be done.

Easy answer: get faster elevators.

So they sent a team of people to research that solution. They needed to know how long it would take to install these elevators, whether they could do them all at once or one at a time, what amount of increased speed was promised by a juiced-up elevator, and, of course, how much this was going to cost.

The numbers came back good. They could fix one elevator at a time over the course of three to four months and reduce wait time by about fifteen to twenty seconds. It would only cost eight million dollars. The leadership team was pleased. This was a doable project with a reasonable budget. The tenants would be thrilled with the faster elevators. It looked like they were going to sign this contract for rocket elevators, until one of the junior executives asked a couple of questions.

"Are the elevators broken?" No.

"Are our elevators slower than any other regular elevator?" No.

"Okay, so are we even solving the right problem?" (Silence.)

The investigative team was given an instruction to find another solution. After a couple of weeks of heavy research, they came back to the executives and reported that they had a different approach— mirrored doors. Apparently their tenants were simply impatient. If they could distract these people with a full-length mirror for fifteen to twenty seconds, they wouldn't even notice the wait time.

This option would only take two months and cost $60,000.

Y'all! They saved *eight million dollars* by asking better questions and not accepting the first solution. It didn't matter that they had the eight million to spend in the first place, the second option was better.

"Working hard is important," says McKeown. "But more effort does not necessarily yield more results. 'Less but better' does."[59]

McKeown's whole book explains this "less but better" mentality. He gives dozens of anecdotes about focusing on what matters and ignoring everything else. A common way of thinking about this is the Pareto Principle: 80 percent of our results come from 20 percent of our work.[60] It might sound like this principle contradicts my earlier statement that the little things matter, but it doesn't, and here's why. Not all little things are important, but the ones that are important are *really* important. Remember brushing your teeth ...

To come up with a "less but better" solution, you have to start by interrogating the problem. This starts with the obvious question: what's the problem? Several answers will jump out at you. Good, write those down. Then go one step further. I want you to cross-examine the problem. Revert to your five-year-old self and ask "why?" (ad nauseum). I want you to make the problem give up all of its secrets and present you with the truest essence of itself.

If asking more questions isn't working, go investigate the problem in person. Put on your Indiana Jones hat, grab a whip, and head into the wilds. Explore the problem from other angles. Make notes about everything you see, but also make notes about everything that is missing. You'll start to see the bigger picture, and this, my friend, is where we want to be.

We want to see the big picture and come up with real solutions. When we know what the real problem is—not what you saw the first time, but the actual problem—we can address it. When I got stuck on the bench press, it seemed like I had just taken on too much too soon. That wasn't the problem; the problem was that I didn't have a spotter to help me get the weight back up. When all of my coworkers quit, the problem seemed to be lack of time and too much work. That wasn't the problem, either, but I knew enough to look for better answers. The solution was to let go of the nonessential, automate where I could, and focus all of my available time on what was most important.

By asking better questions, you can get a full understanding of the issue. Once you can see that clearly, you can create a permanent fix. You don't have to accept easy answers. You don't have to keep fighting the same battles. You can create lasting change that brings out your best, and probably do it without working harder.

CHAPTER 16

I Can Fix Everything

think everyone has an annoying superpower. Something you do that creates remarkable results but drives other people crazy in the process. My brother is unnervingly calm. He doesn't get excited about anything, but he doesn't get upset about anything either. A typical response to any life-changing information is "hmm." This makes him a great listener and a good devil's advocate in arguments, because he's not usually attached to either side.

My husband is insatiably curious. He has to know things. They don't have to be important things, although he has to know those too. He just has to know. Almost all of the time, this superpower is incredibly useful. It means I don't have to remember much of anything, because he will either already know or will find the answer in less than five minutes. The rest of the time, it's just annoying because he's scrolling the interwebs trying to figure out what town we were in when we saw that gigantic farmhouse on the side of the road.

My annoying superpower is that I have to make things better. It's a compulsion. Even if the house is spotless, I can find a crumb to sweep away, a baseboard to dust, or stack of something to tidy. It's the reason I write and rewrite and rewrite. I know I can do better. Even at my day job, I have to meddle in things and try to find efficiencies or process improvements. Lucky for me, my boss is cool with the meddling and usually approves all of my little initiatives.

Sometimes the meddling gets away from me, and I start meddling with other people's lives. My brother and I lived together for a couple of years. He was nervous about moving in with me because I come across as a little—ahem—high-strung. I needed a roommate, and he needed a room. So it made sense for us to cohabitate. It wasn't long before I started meddling in his life and trying to improve his processes.

His chill attitude extends to things like work, food, and laundry. He was employed, but I knew he could be doing more. I kept trying to push him to get a better job. You know, one that paid more and had banking hours. He said he was happy doing what he was doing and he'd get around to making a resume eventually. I tried to coach him to make healthy eating choices and meal prep for the week. He said it was easier to just nuke some ramen and call it a day. I tried to explain that if he washed his linens every weekend, he'd get to start the week with fresh towels and crisp bedsheets. He said he washed his towels once they started to smell funky. He is an adult and he hasn't died. So I suppose his way is working. It's not optimal, but it's functional.

He eventually moved out and got to keep his place the way he wanted. Would you believe that all of my helpful mentorship didn't take? His favorite food is still ramen (a diet staple). I'm pretty sure he doesn't have a budget, resume, or list of goals for the year. And I'm not even going to ask about the towels.

My brother's superpower probably evens out my superpower in this example. Because he's so unbelievably laid-back, he puts up with all of my mothering and still loves me. I'm so grateful for our relationship, even if he doesn't follow any of my advice.

The lie: **I can fix everything.**

---

* * *

How I squashed the lie:

Not everyone I try to fix has taken it as well as my brother. Several years ago I was dating someone pretty seriously. I joked that I liked him because he was exactly how I liked my tea: strong, southern, and sweet. He also had these dreamy blue eyes that would stop you dead in your tracks. Pause for a sec: can we just all be upset together that so many pairs of good eyelashes and eyebrows are wasted on men? I have to coax my brows and lashes out of hiding with the careful application of makeup. This guy had no appreciation for how good he had it with his peepers.

That wasn't the only thing he didn't appreciate. He was an incredibly content person. Actually, now that I'm reflecting, he was a lot like my brother. He was happy with his job, working in a small town. He liked his coworkers and customers, and he made enough money to get by. He never considered doing anything else. Then I came along with my endless ambition and my constant need for improvement and went to work on him. I pulled all my usual tricks to make his life better.

I got him to change his diet and start working out. What started from my helpful nagging turned into a passion for him. In six months he did a Captain America-style transformation. Only instead of putting on fifty pounds of muscle, he took off seventy-five pounds of fat. His peak physique showed up in time for summer, and I was the big-time winner of the hottest boyfriend award. A couple of times when we were out in public, I caught other women ogling him. I was so proud. My encouragement had worked.

It didn't work anywhere else, though. I tried to get him to be more ambitious at work. There was a management position opening up in another town, and he was on the shortlist for the promotion. He didn't want it, because it meant moving farther away from his family. I tried to explain logic like cars and weekends to him, to no avail. He told his boss he didn't want the job, and they passed him over. I was furious. He had an opportunity to increase his experience, advance his career, and make more money, and he turned it down for Wednesday night dinner with his mom?! This made no sense to me.

We started fighting. Small fights at first, but eventually really nasty ones with name-calling. It was in one of these fights that I learned he believed a woman's place was in the home. He thought my ambition was an unbecoming quality in a woman. He didn't understand why I couldn't just be happy. Even worse, he had a warped sense of the word "submission." We were both raised in church, and there is a verse in the New Testament about wives being submissive to their husbands (Ephesians 5:22). If I wanted to be his wife, I had to understand that God had appointed him head of the household and I was not supposed to argue with him ever. I would not be allowed to manage or even view the finances. I was supposed to blindly accept his decisions for our family, financial situation, and future. He was furious that we even had this argument. He thought I should know better.

I explained to him that God made me intelligent and that by not thinking for myself I was not honoring my gift. If God gave me a brain, I was darn well going to use it. If I had opinions, I was going to voice them. The Bible doesn't say, "Wives, always accept your husband's opinions, will, and whims as law. Never think for yourself." I've looked. I can't find that scripture anywhere.

After months of bickering about what the future held for us, we parted ways. I was never going to be the submissive woman he wanted, and he wasn't going to suddenly develop some ambition or agree with gender equality.

Our breakup hurt. I had pretty big feelings for him, and they were wasted because he couldn't see the error of his ways. He wouldn't let me help him. He was going to live a small life in a small town and keep his small-minded ideals.

I thought that if I read enough books on relationships, I could figure out a way to fix him and salvage what we had. The message in every relationship book was "you can't fix other people; you can only fix yourself." It only took fifteen or sixteen of these books to make me reevaluate my position.

We simply had different values and expectations. Although I still like to think mine are better than his, they are not. I don't get to decide what other people want. He wanted a comfortable job where he liked what he did and who he worked with. He wanted to be near his family, because having a strong relationship with them was important. He wanted a woman who would support his choices and not nag him to be anything other than who he was. There's nothing wrong with any of that. It was just not a life I could fit into. So I let him go.

* * *

How you can squash it too:

I remember the first time I found out not everything was fixable. I was four years old, and my greatest treasure was a snow globe my parents had brought home from some trip. I carried this thing with me everywhere. It went to preschool with me and outside to the sandbox. It even slept on my nightstand.

Family friends from out of town came for a visit. They had a daughter who was about a year younger than I was. She thought my snow globe was very cool. I showed her how to turn it upside down to make the snow float and how to turn the crank at the bottom to make music play. She wanted to try it herself, and in the process of trying to get the music to play, she dropped it. The glass shattered on the floor. I didn't panic; I knew just what to do. I grabbed the base and the biggest pieces of glass and walked into the living room where our parents were talking. I handed the shards to my dad and asked him to fix it.

It broke my heart when he told me he couldn't fix it. They tried buying me a replacement, plastic this time, but it wasn't the same.

You can't fix everything. I think, as humans, we are hardwired to help. We hear a crying baby or a whining dog, and we want to soothe them. We see an old lady struggling across the road and we want to give her a hand. We hear about someone's tragic loss and we want to shower them with love, bring them dinner, or send them a card. We are helpers. But helping and fixing are not the same thing, and there are times when "helping" isn't helpful.

Trying to fix someone else or their problems falls into the realm of things you can't control. Author Gabby Bernstein shared three tips about what to do when you want to fix someone else's problems:[61]

1. Remember that your way isn't always the best way. Gabby calls this respecting other people's "guidance systems." What works for you won't work for everyone, and what works for everyone won't always work for you. You have to accept that other people are going to value things differently and choose a course of action that aligns with those values and beliefs. Inserting your beliefs or values into someone else's life doesn't fix a problem; it makes one. For an example of this, see the story of my failed romance above.

2. Allow people to make mistakes. Gabby calls this "not depriving people of hitting bottom." This one is even harder than the first tip, because you can probably see the bottom someone is going to crash into. You want to spare them the pain and misery, but that's not your job. When the bottom comes for them, you have to let it. This doesn't apply to things like letting toddlers touch hot stove burners; it's more like letting the chick get out of its own egg.

3. People who don't want to change won't, and there's nothing you can do about it. Amen.

Gabby goes on to suggest that instead of trying to fix people, you learn to love and accept them as they are. I could not agree more. It's going to take some discernment on your part to know when your help is helpful and when it isn't, but I think that by truly respecting others you will find this balance.

If you are a born fixer, like me, you don't have to stop fixing. There are loads of things that could probably use a good fix and are 100 percent in your control. Here are some examples:

- your opinion of yourself and your work,
- your actions and reactions,
- what you say (to yourself and others),
- how you treat yourself (and others),
- your effort,
- your attitude,
- where you put your energy, and
- your environment.

Fixing what you can, keeping yourself right, and loving other people where they're at are the best ways to make things better.

CHAPTER 17

I'll Get to It Eventually

IN second grade I wrote my first poem. It was about ducks on a pond. There's a joke in there somewhere about a word that rhymes with duck, but I'm going to let it slide. For the first time ever, I had learned to express myself on paper, and I did really well. The teacher told my parents I had a gift. From that day on, I knew I wanted to be a writer.

Other kids were good at art, singing, or sports. Me, I was good at writing. Poetry was my thing for a long time. I submitted original poems to school competitions and always came in the top three. The whole tortured poet vibe went well with my angsty teen attitude in high school.

Then I got into college, and my parents told me I was a decent writer but there was no way I could make money doing something creative. I had to get a job after graduation, and I needed to pick something practical to major in. They were hoping for something like pharmacy or engineering. Those weren't my style. Much to my parents' dismay, I majored in economics. I tried to say that econ was the science of business, but no one bought that (I still think I'm a little right).

When I went to college, I had this beautiful life plan worked out. I would major in creative writing and write my first book by the end of school. Then I would BE a writer. I'd have a beautiful office with a big executive desk right in the middle of the floor, matching executive chair and credenza included. The walls would be lined with built-in bookshelves stuffed with books. I would always have a steaming cup of coffee, and I'd sit there every morning in the fresh light of day, surrounded by creativity, working on my newest manuscript.

When I changed my major to economics, the vision for the future changed, but the dream remained. Instead of becoming a writer first thing, I'd have to use the back door. I would be a business tycoon by day and a writer by night. Instead of the office library, I'd work from a kitchen table, scribbling desperately into a notebook in the dark after-dinner hours. But I'd do it.

Homework and work-work got in the way of my writing in college. Then it was just work-work and adulting that got in the way of writing. People stopped asking what I wanted to do with my life, but I knew I was a writer. I told anyone who would listen that I was going to write a book. Small problem—I had no idea what I was going to write about. So even when I could have found time to write, I didn't. It was hard to come up with an idea worthy of my debut novel.

I said I was going to write a book for more than ten years before I actually did it. I started books a couple of times, either fiction or nonfiction. My first idea was called *Winning with Men*; it was collection of stories from my misadventures in love. After a couple of chapters, I realized it wasn't funny and it was hard to talk about a lot of people without revealing their identities. I didn't want anyone coming after me because I had told the world they were an asshole—even if I was right.

As much as I tout productivity and efficiency and following dreams, I was procrastinating and leaving my dream out in the cold. I never, ever considered that I wouldn't write a book, but I wasn't going to do it now. I'd write when I had a better idea. I'd write when I had more time. I'd write when things calmed down in my personal life. I'd write after I got a promotion...

The lie: **I'll get to it eventually.**

***

How I squashed the lie:

If you were to look at my goal lists for the past ten years, you would see "write a book" at the top of the list. Yes, I wanted to run half-marathons, go to Paris, lose fifteen pounds, get a promotion, get my MBA, get a Kate Spade bag, and read one hundred books per year. But the big, hairy, audacious goal was always to write a book.

But every time I went to write, something else popped up that was more important. There was a crisis. My stepdad had a stroke and I needed to be there for my family. Or my sister was getting married and I needed to prioritize my maid of honor duties over writing. Amazon shopping for party decorations and bridesmaid dresses had to come first. Sometimes it was a work crisis. The executive I worked for needed something yesterday, and I was the only one who could make it happen. Or maybe it wasn't a crisis, but just a big project at work that required all of my attention, even in nonwork hours.

And then it was my MBA. The MBA was demanding of my time, and if I did have free time I needed to focus on other people so no one would feel neglected. There was nothing left over for writing. If it wasn't work, my family, or my MBA, it was something else.

Then something happened that changed everything. I took a Dale Carnegie self-development course offered through work. Part of this program was (required) one-on-one coaching calls with the Dale Carnegie rep. This guy was awesome. He was well-spoken, fun, and full of relevant advice that helped. On one of our calls, he asked about my goals, and I told him I wanted to write a book. We unpacked that I was procrastinating because I didn't think my dream was more important than my other life commitments. I was going to start, but I was going to start once everything calmed down.

He reminded me that life never calms down. It's always one thing or another. If it weren't, I'd have already written the book. All it took to be a writer was my butt in the chair, my fingers on the keys, and some focused effort. My family, job, community, and friends could live without me for half an hour a day. The world would not implode. Monday magic wasn't going to help me. I needed to start today. I needed to stop waiting for tomorrow.

He was right. So I decided to write a first draft in fourteen days. It didn't have to be good. It didn't have to change lives. It didn't have to even be coherent. It had to be complete. For two weeks I could put myself and my dreams first and see what happened. I didn't finish in fourteen days—I finished in eight.

* * *

How you can squash it too:

How many times a week do you say to yourself, "That's it, I'm getting my shit together!" And you mean it. No taksie backsies. Today is the day!

And then your cat pukes on the carpet. You spill coffee all over yourself and have to change, again. You're late to work. Your boss needs something by noon, but you're scheduled for back-to-back meetings all day. The school calls and your kid is sick. Now your pet and your kid are puking. Awesome. You're taking work calls from the couch while your kid ralphs in the next room. Between work calls, you text your husband and ask him to pick up some ground beef and milk on his way home. By the end of the work day you're exhausted, but the kid is finally sleeping. Your husband shows up without said grocery items. You have to order pizza again. There goes your diet … Today is clearly *not* the day you are going to get your shit together. Tomorrow, though—tomorrow is definitely the day.

There are five reasons why you aren't getting to your goals faster:

1. **You don't have time.** We already know life likes to intervene when we are trying to do something bigger. Even if you've set aside time to do something for yourself or your goals, someone else's needs creep in and steal it. You are

already doing everything—how can you possibly add time for anything else?

2. **It's hard.** You are already tired and don't have the energy for anything else right now. Plus, if you were meant to have that body/that job/those friends, it would naturally come to you. You're trying to force things into your life that don't want to be there. It shouldn't be so hard.

3. **It's uncomfortable.** Working on something isn't fun. You knew exactly how to get through the maze to get the cheese and then here's a new thing. It's a new maze. You have to learn how to navigate it, and why would you do that when you already know how to get the cheese in the old maze?

4. **You aren't sure the results will be worth it.** Why bother stepping out of your comfort zone and doing hard things if you can't be sure it will work? What if you spend all this time putting yourself first and then you find out that your husband is mad at you for neglecting your marriage? Your kid is upset that you missed one of their twenty weekly practices for their five sports. Your boss thinks you don't need the distractions. Is what you want so important that you have to put yourself first? What will happen to everyone else?

5. **You're the only one doing it.** None of your friends are doing hard things. They are content with their current lives. They don't understand why you can't just be happy. Doing things alone makes them twice as hard.

"You can't be committed to your own bullshit and your growth. It's one or the other," says author Scott Stabile.[62] Every one of those excuses is bullshit. I'm calling you on them. Not only do you deserve to live the life you want, you *need* to do it.

Getting what you want starts with determining what you want. For most of us, that isn't a problem. We can identify what could be better in our lives. Promotion, respect, different figure, nicer car/house/clothes, more money, successful side hustle—scratch that, successful mega business, more followers, luscious garden, clean house, adoring children, doting husband. Basically, living the life you dream about instead of the one you have.

The next step is figuring out what you need to do to get those things and starting. I know it seems sexier to start on a Monday, or on the first of the month, or better yet on New Year's Day. You buy into the nonsense that says starting something new on the first day of the week/month/year will be the secret ingredient that ensures *this time* you make it.

Let me ask you something: Do you actually want what you think you want? What if I told you that you can have 10 million dollars, a hot body, a loving family, and never have to work again, *but* you have to pick up the money next Tuesday. Are you going to tell me I need to hold that money for six days so your life can change on a Monday? No. You are going to march yourself to wherever I tell you and get that money into your hot little hands as soon as possible. I bet you'll even be early.

If the results were waiting for you to just come and get them, there would be nothing that could stand in your way. Not a sick kid, stained clothing, work, or your spouse. Nope. None of it would phase you, because you would be walking into your dream. I'm not saying you can't take care of your family, career, or marriage. I'm just saying there's a point when you have to stop letting yourself down.

If I had to guess, you are the kind of person who will go out of their way to help someone else. You will make a midnight Walmart run to get poster board for your child's project they *just* remembered is due tomorrow. You'll rearrange your entire schedule to fit in whatever your boss decides to throw at you. You find out your friend is having a rough time and you'll go grab Starbucks and drive across town to make sure they have everything they need. This is admirable; don't change any of these things.

But again, when do you make time for you? When do your goals get to be a priority? When do you get to work on your dreams? You can't finish something if you never start. Success doesn't come from what you do occasionally. It comes from what you do consistently. A little bit of effort here and there won't cut it.

Here are some reasons you need to kick procrastination in the pants:

1. **For your family.** Your family deserves the best of you. Not the person you wish you could be if only you had time. No, they deserve your best. In order to be your best, you have to stop catering to the tyranny of the urgent. You need to set some boundaries in your life and give yourself space to grow. If you can do that and still be home for a hot meal every night, God bless. You go, girl. But if you need to take some of the energy you've put toward your family and refocus it on being a healthier, wealthier, better you—do it. Don't apologize. Explain to your family what you're doing and why. Ask for their support. Most importantly, tell them what they will get at the end of it.

2. **For your career.** The way you do anything is the way you do everything. When you allow other people to put you last, you have decided that last place is acceptable. Last place effort is okay. You can't possibly bring your best to the table when you

aren't taking care of yourself. It seems counterintuitive to say that by putting yourself first you'll be able to do better at work, but you will. You won't become better and then say, "Nah, I'm not bringing my better self to work today. I'll bring the old me there and schlep through." That's ridiculous. If you start feeling better about yourself, you'll bring a better attitude, better energy, and more creative ideas everywhere you go.

3. **For the future.** You can't have the future you want unless you do the things right now that will take you there. If you don't save for retirement, you won't be off traveling the world. If you don't take care of your body, it could get sick or give out before you're ready. You have to prepare for the things you want to come to pass, but preparation without action won't make them happen. Enable your future to be brighter for yourself and the people you care about.

4. **For others.** You can't pour out of an empty cup. Putting yourself last means that you get whatever is left over. What remains after you've taken care of everyone and everything else is a pitiful portion. You then have exactly that portion to work with the next time you need to pour into someone's life. This is no good for you or them. You want to bless other people and deliver what they need from you. Good! If you want to give them your best, you have to first have enough to give.

5. **For yourself.** Putting yourself first is not selfish. It's not egotistical. It doesn't mean you don't love other people. It means you love them enough to be better for them. More importantly, it means you care enough about your life, future, and happiness that you are willing to put in the work to do it beautifully.

Now that that's settled, what is going to change? Are you going to wait until Monday to start something, or are you going to start now? Monday magic will not make your goals more achievable. The reason we don't start is usually because other people's urgent issues get in the way. You want to be a good parent, friend, employee, neighbor. So when they come calling for your time, and they always will, you allow them to take priority. I would never suggest that you neglect your responsibilities. But you should consider yourself and your goals an equal priority. By taking care of yourself and your dreams, you enable the best version of you to be available for all the others who need you. Creating the life you dream about will create more joy in you. Name one thing that is made worse by joy. I'll wait.

CHAPTER 18

Someone Else's Success Means My Failure

I used to believe that success was a zero-sum game. The concept of zero-sum games comes from the study of economics and game theory. It's one of the easiest games to understand, because the rules are simple. Your gain is equal to your opponent's loss or vice versa. When you were a kid and you had to flip a coin to determine who got to pick the cereal for the week, you either won or you lost. There's no compromise in a coin toss. It's heads or tails, and if you pick wrong you lose.

When I lost I got really focused on the losing. I would become obsessive about how to not lose in the future. I would make irrational decisions to compensate for my losses. It wasn't just the pain of losing that was a problem, it was the aftermath that followed. Seems pretty intense for not getting to pick the family cereal, right?

A good example of this was when I doing strategy for a C-level executive. In order to move ahead professionally, you have to do two things: do good work and get that work noticed by the right people. Doing good work in the dark won't get you ahead. Someone, in some kind of position of power, has to see your work, like your work, and want more of it. That's all moving up the corporate ladder is.

Working for a C-level executive gave me the opportunity to get my work noticed, and I was doing good work. But I had another coworker who always beat me out for the good project, got invited to important meetings, and received recognition from people who mattered. This person was dressed well, highly educated, and had a tremendous amount of experience. It's only natural that our leadership would always ask for their opinion, give them the most challenging projects, and invite them to be our team representative in meetings. Because of those opportunities, they were always going to move ahead faster and farther than me.

Every time they got assigned to lead the next major initiative or were asked to present to a group of executives, I felt like my career was under attack. There was one person who got to lead the project. If it wasn't me, it was them. If they won, I lost.

I claim temporary insanity for the next part of the story. I started making crazed choices about how to get ahead at work. I spent money I didn't have on a wardrobe upgrade. I thought I needed to look the part if I was going to be taken seriously. I started taking on more work than was necessary, because I felt like it might make a difference. At the end of the day, I ended up stressed out, in debt, and frustrated because my coworker got the promotion anyway.

There's a great NPR article by Shankar Vedantam called "How

the 'Scarcity Mindset' Can Make Problems Worse."[63] It does a great job of explaining how perceived losses lead to poor choices. "When you really want something, you start to focus on it obsessively," says Vedantam. "When you're hungry, it's hard to think of anything other than food, when you're desperately poor, you constantly worry about making ends meet. Scarcity produces a kind of tunnel vision, and it explains why, when we're in a hole, we often lose sight of long-term priorities and dig ourselves even deeper."

Vedantam goes on to say that it's not the loss, necessarily, that's the problem. It's the obsession surrounding the loss that causes desperate, impulsive decisions focusing on the immediate and ignoring the larger picture. When a bill collector comes calling and you're short on money, you'll do whatever you have to do to get them off your back. But what about feeding your family next week, or paying the other bills coming up? Those thoughts never cross your mind, because you can't see beyond the "past due" yelling in your face.

A scarcity mentality can impact any area of your life. It showed up in my love life, my career, and my finances. If someone got engaged, it meant there was one less potential romantic partner for me. I would throw myself into the dating pool and start seeing large numbers of people in order to ensure I got a partner before they were all gone. If someone got promoted at work, it meant they limited my career growth. On more than one occasion when this happened, I felt like I *needed* to start at a new company to save my future. I would send out hundreds of resumes in a short period of time, go on dozens of interviews, and basically take the same job at a different company. When money got tight, I started making even worse financial choices. I would stop saving and start pouring all of my money into the problem. I would buy cheap instead of buying quality and then I would end up needing to buy three to four times as much, which meant even tighter situations. These were self-perpetuating loss cycles.

The lie: someone else's success means my failure.

---

* * *

How I squashed the lie:

Scarcity seems scary, because it limits your perspective. It focuses on the "not enough" and blinds you to alternative ways of looking at the situation. When you can't see another way out, you feel trapped and start making desperate decisions.

At one point I was $30,000 in debt and freaking out. I had a bad case of scarcity mindset and ended up making the situation worse before I made it better. I did things like taking on more debt, taking money out of my savings, and picking up extra hours at work. When those things weren't enough, I severely cut back my spending, sold half of my belongings, and rented out my bedroom on Airbnb. I did eventually get to a place where I broke even, but it was hard and my quality of life sucked.

I knew going into my MBA program that I would have to take out student loans to pay for it. I thought that when I graduated with my MBA, I would be rewarded with a promotion and a salary increase that would cover the cost of those loans. But when time for my promotion came up, the position went to one of my coworkers and I was stuck making my same salary. I already functioned on a slim budget, so there was no room to cut anything unless I wanted to try eating only every other day. This time, instead of freaking out and behaving irrationally, I thought about my position and tried to expand my options. I could get a second job, but that would be hard since I worked until six most nights and retail or restaurant shifts usually start earlier. I could find another job, which could take a while but was doable. Or I could do something really big and sell my house.

I did some calculations and figured out there was enough appreciation on my house to pay off my loans and still have more than my initial down payment left over. I loved my house, but I hated the thought of going back into debt, and there was no way my current salary could support the monthly payments. So I downsized to a really nice apartment and paid off my loans. It wasn't a luxury apartment, but it was well maintained and had decent amenities. I have never regretted this decision, and it allowed me the opportunity to find an even better home a year later.

Instead of panicking I got creative. When my promotion vanished, I found other options. I would love to tell you that when my coworker got the promotion my first response was congratulatory. It wasn't. Just like I had to shift my perspective to find the answer to my money problems, I had to shift my perspective to be happy for my coworker. I'm not perfect but I figured out a healthier and more productive way to respond. Now when other people win, I don't see a loss. I see an opportunity for a gain.

I found three things that happen when people achieve their goals that make things better for everyone.

1. **They prove it can be done.** When we see other people
    do something, it increases our belief that we can do it too. In
    the 1950s there were many runners trying to break a four-
    minute-mile pace. No one had ever done it before, and many
    athletes made attempts and failed. Scientists even performed
    conclusive studies showing that due to the physical limita-
    tions of the human body it was impossible for anyone to run
    a mile in less than four minutes. Then Roger Bannister did
    the impossible. He ran a full mile in 3 minutes 59.4 seconds.
    People were dumbfounded. Since then fourteen hundred
    men have also broken a four-minute mile.[64] No woman has
    broken that record yet (as far as I know), but I have full confi-
    dence that many will. Bannister's run wasn't a fluke, it was fuel
    for the rest of the speed demons out there. It's true no one else
    could be the first to break the limit, but their mile times are no
    less valid. Personally, if I could break a fifteen-minute mile, I
    would feel pretty speedy.

2. **They create more opportunities.** When other people do
    things, they create subsequent opportunities for everyone else.
    When someone gets the lead role in a movie, the movie will
    need actors, stylists, directors, producers, and countless other
    support staff. The lead has gone to someone, but opportunity
    is ripe for the taking. If your enemy gets a huge promotion and
    a new house, their old house is now available for someone else
    and their new house will need professionals to service it, creat-
    ing work for people. What about when someone gets a new
    customer? Sure, that's one less customer in the world for your
    competitive business. BUT, every time someone sells a new
    account, they increase awareness of your product/service/

industry. Their sale does not preclude you from capitalizing on the additional exposure their sale has created.

3. **They can help you.** This one is tricky, because it means you have to be humble enough to ask for help. If you're mad at them for doing something you want to do, you'll miss out on the invaluable experience they can share. I have a physical and psychological *need* to ask people how they lost weight. If I see someone post anywhere that they've lost ten, twenty, fifty, two hundred pounds, I want to know how they did it. I have already read hundreds of articles and dozens of books on weight loss. I have hired personal trainers who coached me on my own health decisions. I have been a member of seven gyms in my area (not at the same time). I already know how to lose weight. This doesn't stop me from complimenting them on their accomplishment and asking them how they did it. I am severely disappointed that no one has yet told me, "The secret is napping and milkshakes."

People love to tell you what worked for them and how they overcame. I would bet all five dollars in my wallet that most people would be happy to tell you how they achieved your goals. You may even get the one nugget of advice that rockets you to the finish line.

***

How you can squash it too:

You don't lose anything when others win, and you don't win anything when others lose. When you begrudge someone their achievements, you put more negativity into your life and stifle your own efforts. When you look for the good, you get more good and you enhance your efforts. It's the difference between running uphill and running downhill. Don't make things harder for yourself by being ugly. I hate to tell you this, but people are going to create lives they love whether you approve of them doing it or not. They are going to win even if it means pissing you off. They will succeed and won't even consider that it might hurt your feelings. When these things happen, it doesn't mean less for you. It can mean more, if you choose to focus on the abundance and not the lack.

Here are five ways to start thinking in terms of abundance instead of scarcity:

1. **Change your perspective.** You are a rational human being completely capable of making good decisions and seeing things for what they are. When scarcity tries to tell you there isn't enough, flip the script and see how less is more. "There isn't enough money" can become "there are gazillions of dollars out there; I just have to figure out how to get a little more of them."

2. **Think creatively.** Let the lack inspire your creative genius to come up with possibilities. The front door is locked. Did you try the back door? Can you push open a window? Can you break a window and safely crawl through? Does a neighbor have a key? Are you even at the right house? When the solution you wanted isn't available, find other solutions. Explore the full depth and breadth of alternatives.

3. **Make someone else's win your win.** Figure out how to make everything that seems like a win/lose situation into a win/win situation. This will take some creativity, but it can

be done. The key is figuring out the interests of everyone involved and working to find solutions that address some or all of those interests. Better to get something than accept a total loss.

4. **Celebrate the now.** Maybe you missed an opportunity, but that doesn't mean you went backward. What is good about where you are? At one point you wanted to be here instead of somewhere else. Try to remember what was so good about being here in the first place. Being grateful, even if you still dream of bigger things, is a way to weaken scarcity.

5. **Focus on your strengths, not your weaknesses.** I heard author John Maxwell give a talk once encouraging people to pour their energy into making their strengths better instead of trying to fix their weaknesses. If you're constantly working on your weaknesses, you're throwing all your energy at getting something bad to be tolerable. If you focus on your strengths instead, you'll make your best even better. You're allowed to have shortcomings and to try to improve them, but the biggest successes come from playing from a position of power. When you feel strong, it's easier to see opportunities.

When you feel the anxiety of scarcity start to creep in, just remember that it's not a fact, it's a perspective. You can change it and get better outcomes. Giving in to the scarcity mindset only makes your world smaller and your decisions worse. I absolutely believe there is abundance and opportunity lurking behind every corner. Y'all, there is so, so much in the world. It's right there waiting for you to take it. But first you have to train yourself to see it.

CHAPTER 19

If I Could Just ___, I'd Be Happy

I just want my extra weight to fall off me and turn into cash. —Unknown

IF I could just lose this last twenty pounds. If I could just get that promotion. If I could have a new car. When we buy a house. When I'm married. When I have kids. When my kids are potty-trained. When they are out of the house. When I finish my book. When they publish my book. When people *buy* my book. When my savings account hits $XXX,XXX. When I retire. If I could just visit this one place. If I could just buy that thing. THEN I'll be happy.

Sound familiar? Yeah, I do this all the time. If I could just (whatever), things will be different and I will be happy. We love to believe this lie. It sounds almost like a goal, so it seems safe enough. These little phrases are a combination of procrastination and idealization. You paint a picture of how your life will change for the better when you've finally hit your goal.

- You can relax.
- Your stress will vanish.
- People will find you more attractive.
- You will be awesome at your job.
- You'll feel great.
- You'll finally get to do what you want.
- Your relationships will get better.
- You will know your purpose.
- You'll be content.

Several years ago I found an old notebook where I'd written some goals. These weren't my "annual ten things I want to accomplish in the next year" goals. No, these were my bucket list stretch goals. The third item on that list was making fifty thousand per year in salaried income. I remembered writing this goal and thinking that if I could get to that number, all of my financial worries would disappear and I'd be living the good life. When I found this notebook, I was making more than fifty thousand and my life was basically the same as it was when I was making less. There were a few small improvements, like my subscription to Netflix, but for all intents and purposes, my life had not gotten better.

The lie: I need to do something I'm not doing to be happy.

***

How I squashed the lie:

The last semester of my MBA program got a little crazy. I was taking the most classes ever, my job was demanding, and I sold my house and moved. I was busy, but I knew that all of these things were coming to an end. I was going to get my degree in two months, my projects at work were coming to a close, and once I finished that stupid move it would be over. Then what?

I wouldn't have any big goals or big projects to keep me occupied. I'd be alone with my thoughts and time. I hadn't had time since I started my MBA program, and I wasn't sure if I'd like going from a hundred miles per hour to stalled. So I started researching next steps. I was in a really good groove with this whole school thing, so why not just keep going. I could get my PhD in strategy and be Dr. Nikki Soulsby. It has a nice ring to it, eh?

I gave my best sales pitch of this idea to my boyfriend, and I will never forget the look on his face when I finished. He's an incredibly supportive, patient man. But in this instance, he furrowed his brows and asked me why I couldn't just be happy for five minutes? I was finishing a grueling eighteen-month program at a top-ranked university. I had worked my ass off from dawn till nearly midnight, and I wasn't even going to appreciate my own achievement? I was going to blow past all of that work and start something else?

He wasn't exactly a fan of this idea, but he did have some solid points. What would happen if I tried to just be happy in the moment? What if I (*gulp*) took a couple of months off and relaxed?

I did not apply to the PhD program, but I did manage to find joy in my achievement and learn to relax. No one will ever accuse me of being chill, but I have figured out how to be grateful for my life—for what it is, what it was, and what it will be.

* * *

How you can squash it too:

Carina Wolff from *Bustle* wrote an article about seven things that won't make you happy according to science.[65]

1. **Buying stuff.** This might give you a temporary high, but it always leaves you wanting more. Instead of having new things, aim to experience new things.

2. **More money.** Research shows that making over seventy-five thousand a year will not make you happy. As your earnings increase past this number, you get a smaller marginal increase in happiness. When you're making a million per year, another ten thousand doesn't even phase you. You'll take it, but it won't make you happier.

3. **Fame.** Instead of creating happiness, it tends to generate stress—primarily from lack of privacy and unrealistic expectations. What does makes you happy is confidence in yourself.

4. **Living in a big city.** We like to think that cities like New York and Los Angeles are full of hope and dreams, but the people there are scientifically less happy. The massive cost of living, increased crime rates, constant noise, and lack of space start to grate after a while. So maybe Hallmark is onto something and quaint towns are where it's at.

5. **Having a hot partner.** Apparently couples unequally yoked in the looks department are more likely to face insecurities. This is why people generally end up with partners

around their same level of attractiveness. I can tell you first-hand that security in my relationship is way better than a six-pack, but I won't turn down both.

6. **Long vacations.** "Studies show that a two-week vacation is just as gratifying as a week-long one." I guess this is a case where less is more, since you'll be able to remember your experiences better in a shorter time frame.

7. **Having lots of sex.** More isn't better here either. There was a study done at Carnegie Mellon proving that more sex leads to "less happiness, decreased sexual satisfaction, and reduced well-being."[66]

Truth: If you are not happy with what you have now, you won't be any more happy when _____ happens.

I know this seems all wrong. If your dreams came true you'd be pumped ... until they became your new normal. Then the emptiness that causes your unhappiness will resurface and you'll have another round of "I'll be happy when ... "

Stuff, accomplishments, rewards, recognition ... if these things control your happiness, my friend, you are in big trouble. Your happiness is determined primarily by your outlook on life. People who have horrific circumstances find ways to get up every morning and smile. People who have it all can still be miserable.

When you choose to be grateful for what is good in your life, your life gets better. If you choose to focus on what you think you are missing, you'll never, *ever* be happy no matter what you accomplish, what you buy, or how much money you make. Like attracts like, and when you show love to what you have, it shows love back in the form of joy, contentment, and radiance. Who doesn't want to be radiant?

"No matter where you go, there you are." —Buckaroo Banzai[67]

Buckaroo is right. You can't get rid of yourself. You can move. You can get a new job. You can lose weight. You can make more money. You can earn respect. You can change your friends. You can win awards. You can get all of the applause. You can get all of the followers. You can build an empire. And at the end of the day, you are still you, with all of your flaws, insecurities, and shortcomings. You must learn to be happy today, so that when things do get better in the future, you can be happy tomorrow. The easiest way I know how to do this is to start a gratitude practice.

Being grateful doesn't take a long time. In fact, I think you should do it in two scenarios.

1. **While you're drinking your first morning beverage.**
   By this time in the day, your brain should be functional enough to generate some decent ideas. Find something to be grateful for. If you need to start small, do that. You can be grateful that you are breathing, that you woke up this morning, or that you have ankles. I don't know. Come up with something. It will set your day off right.

2. **When shit hits the fan.** Especially when things go left, you should pause and find gratitude. It may seem stupid to search out the good in the middle of chaos, but it's so worth it. This practice helps me from spiraling out when my life turns upside down. Instead of allowing myself to get sucked into the bad, I redirect my energy into the good. The best way to do this is to find any reason this horrible situation could be good for you. There is a seed of greatness in every adversity. Sometimes the challenge takes up too much space and blocks out the good for a while. No problem. In that case find

anything to be grateful for. When everything seems lost and I'm struggling to find something to be grateful for, I usually go for something ridiculous like fuzzy socks or parmesan cheese. Something that will put me in a better frame of mind to count my blessings.

Gratitude is the magic bullet to happiness. It allows you to process your emotions. It enables you to find the good. It is not dependent on anyone else. It brings joy into the now. It shifts your brain into a positive, productive state. It can reframe challenges into opportunities and loss into gain. It even helps you sleep better.

It is a powerful force for good in your life and will lead to a markedly improved future, but it does take time. One single instance of being grateful is not enough to change your brain. This is why people call it developing a gratitude practice. You never really perfect it, but it gets a lot easier and more beneficial as you go.

Once you can be happy anywhere, you will be happy everywhere.

CHAPTER 20

I Am an Exception to All the Good Advice

I would read self-help books and think, *That's true, but it doesn't apply to me.* This went for positive things and negative things. I would hear that you can't do everything you want all at once, and then take it as a personal challenge to become the *one* person who did it all. And I would ... until burnout got me. I would hear that you can't outwork a bad diet and would promptly buy some Krispy Kremes and try to run off the calories. They said it would take time. They said I had to be consistent. They said I had to make an effort. They said I had to control my attitude. They said I had to focus my energy ... and I thought those rules were really good for other people.

I studied success, self-help, relationship, leadership, and spiritual principles for over a decade. I knew the right things to do. I knew how to reframe my problems, set goals, banish self-limiting beliefs, show gratitude, and play to my strengths. But knowing isn't enough. I had to know *and* apply the truth for it to set me free.

I knew the same success principles when I was depressed, in debt, miserable, working at a soul-sucking job, hoping I could pay my bills, certain I didn't deserve love, frustrated that bad things always happened to me, and toying with the idea of not waking up tomorrow. But I wasn't following any of the advice. It was unused knowledge, which is just a waste of brain space.

The lie: I am an exception to all the good advice.

***

How I squashed the lie:

I am a fairly confident person. Even when I was at my lowest, I would have told you that I was brilliant, underpaid, and deserving of better things. The problem was, I didn't believe any of that! I was being strangled by my self-limiting beliefs. I let the lie hide all of the truth I had learned. When I found out I wasn't mean, it shocked me out of my funk. I realized that if I was so wrong about that, I could be wrong about other things. I knew all about self-limiting beliefs and how they crush ambition, and yet I hadn't kicked mine to the curb.

I did unpack all of the lies I'd been telling myself, but it didn't happen overnight. I used one more success principle to help me get to a healthier, wealthier, happier place. I turned all of that good information into good habits.

One of my favorite quotes is "You will never always feel motivated. So, you must learn to be disciplined. (author unknown)"[68] When I'm motivated, I monitor my self-talk, make long-term decisions, focus, show appreciation, do all the little things, practice gratitude, and on and on. It's super easy to do these things when you have the right motivation. When that wears off, and it always does, discipline is how I finish everything.

There are studies that say self-control is like a muscle.[69] You can flex that muscle only so many times per day before it becomes fatigued. As you continue to use the muscle over time, it gets stronger, but like real muscles, the key here is over time. Overuse of self-control leads to taxation. If you're familiar with working out, it's like doing reps until failure. Your first few reps are strong, maybe even easy. The longer you work that muscle group, the more tired it gets. Eventually you can't lift the weight anymore. Your muscles just fail. You have a set amount of self-control "strength" for each day, and once you've used it up it's gone too.

The goal of self-control is to create good habits. As you discipline yourself to do something, you create a habit. Eventually you don't have to think about the behavior modification. It's just what you do. Discipline is only required when you have to actively choose to do something.

There are dozens of good books out there about how to build and maintain habits. A couple of my favorites are *The Power of Habit* by Charles Duhigg and *Better Than Before* by Gretchen Rubin. Through these books, trainings, and trial and error, I've found seven things that have helped me maintain my discipline and develop good habits.

1. **One thing at a time.** One of the traps I often fall into is trying to do too much all at once. I want to be instantly good at everything. So I try to buckle down and improve in multiple areas. This might work for a week or two, but it is not sustainable. Not only do I get decision fatigue, but I burn out and give up on all of my self-improvement goals before I've completed any of them. It's better to focus on one (maybe two) goals and create solid habits before adding more. Focusing on one thing allows you to put more energy into it and get to the habit zone faster.

2. **Start small.** Instead of making dramatic changes to your life all at once, try starting micro-habits. What is the smallest thing you can do to build the habit you want? Do that until you don't have to think about it anymore and then do more. Rinse and repeat until the thing you were working on is now something you do automatically.

I have a friend who wanted to start drinking more water every day. They tried carrying around a liter of water for a while, but eventually they just left it in their car and went back to coffee and Diet Coke at the office. They heard about using baby steps to create habits and made a second attempt. This time they started by putting a cup in their bathroom. Every morning when they brushed their teeth, they saw the tumbler sitting on the counter. A week went by, and they added putting water in the cup and taking a sip before going downstairs for coffee. They did this for two weeks and then tried to drink the whole cup of water before going downstairs. When this was comfortable, they started the process over with carrying an empty water bottle to work in addition to drinking the cup of water in the morning. Now they drink two glasses of water in the morning before

having any coffee and consume two to three liters of water throughout the day. I can't remember a time I've seen them without water.

3. **Do it now.** Newton's first law of motion is applicable to your
    habits: if a body is moving at a constant speed in a straight
    line, it will keep moving in a straight line at constant speed
    unless it is acted upon by a force.[70] Starting now is the best
    way to do it. It might seem easier to start at the beginning
    of the month or beginning of the week, but there is nothing
    special about 1sts or Mondays. They are arbitrary dates. Your
    clean break is anytime you decide to make a change. I started
    writing this book on the 28th of September in the middle of
    the afternoon. It sounded sexier to start writing on October
    1st, but I realized that waiting two days to start my writing
    was not going to improve the quality of the book. Also, none
    of you care what day I start or finish this book, so long as I
    finish it. Don't wait until January 1st to start exercising. Don't
    wait until the weekend to clean your house. You are allowed
    to start anything at any point in time, and my recommen-
    dation is as soon as possible. Put down this book and take a
    micro-step toward your goal.

4. **Track your progress.** Tracking progress can be done in two
    ways. You can track outcomes or effort. Tracking outcomes is
    probably what you do most of the time. You might track how
    many books you read in a year, the number of new custom-
    ers you get in a month, or even the number of followers on
    your Instagram. All of these outcomes come from substeps
    or effort you have to put in. It's not bad to track outcomes.
    Most of the time, it is the most straightforward way to meas-
    ure your progress. But it's not the only way.

Using the same examples above, measuring effort would look like this: Books per year → how many pages did you read today? New customers per month → how many sales calls did you make? How many client visits did you go on? IG followers → How many posts did you put up this week? Videos? Good graphics? Did you interact with anyone else? How many?

Tracking your effort is useful if you aren't getting to results as fast as you expected, or if you like the encouragement of checking things off a list more frequently.

5. **Reward yourself.** Build in rewards for yourself BEFORE and AFTER you hit your goal. These can be things you spend money on, or not. They can be big or small. I like to pick rewards that are in line with my goals. So if I have a goal to save money, I reward myself with things like walks, bubble baths, or a day to myself to read. I sometimes break big goals down into smaller ones and set rewards for each of them. When I wrote this book, I started with one chapter and then took the night off. When I hit 25 percent I had a glass of wine. At 50 percent I went to a local confectionary and bought chocolate fudge. At 75 percent I got a new candle for my office. When I finished the first draft I bought a cute pair of shoes. And when it got published my husband took me out to my favorite restaurant. With other projects I have rewarded myself with literal gold star stickers on my planner pages, a long walk, or a new book. Whatever will help motivate you to reach your goal will work.

6. **Give yourself enough time.** Habits are not formed in a day. It takes anywhere from eighteen to 254 days of consistent effort to create a habit.[71] Starting is usually easiest because it's when your motivation is highest. You're inspired to do

something new. When the motivation wears off, the real discipline development takes over. You have to start doing things because you actively decide to instead of feeling motivated. Eventually you don't have to force yourself to do it anymore. It's just the way it is. Don't get frustrated when it hasn't stuck after the first week.

7. **Forgive yourself.** You will eventually mess up. You'll forget a day, or something will come up and you won't be able to get whatever done. Welcome to life. Creating habits requires discipline and also grace. Just because you skipped a day doesn't mean you start from the beginning. It also doesn't mean you haul off and make counterproductive choices. Maybe you had to work late and now the gym is closed and it's pouring rain so you can't get your workout in today. This doesn't mean you get to skip all of your workouts for the week. It means that life happened today, and you'll do better next time. You don't have to double up on your workout tomorrow to make up for it. You just have to make sure you're moving in the right direction. Another one of my favorite quotes comes from Robert Brault: "Optimist: someone who figures that taking a step backward after taking a step forward is not a disaster, it's a cha-cha."[72] Cha-cha on, my friend.

If you're tired of any part of your life, you can change it. This can start with a "That's It" moment, but it doesn't have to. Maybe you aren't fed up with how things are, because things aren't that bad but they could be better. How you start changing your life isn't important. Making consistent progress toward the life you want is what matters. You make your habits, and your habits make your life. Eventually habits become unconscious and you automatically do things to create the life you want. Nothing is off the table. Imagine the life you want and then go get it.

* * *

How you can squash it too:

You've just spent a couple of hours reading about the lies I told myself that held me back and the truths that helped me move on. I hope along the way you learned something that can help you achieve your dreams and create a life you love. I hope you are going to love yourself and other people more. I believe you can overcome your own mental monsters and unleash your awesomeness on the world. The world needs you.

You now know these things:

- You don't have to accept what other people say about you as truth.
- You do deserve it.
- Other people can't ruin you.
- You can be good at your job even if you have sucky coworkers, no training, or bad managers.
- Preparing for the future is important.
- You don't need to lose or gain a pound—you're perfect at your own size.
- You don't have to wake up early to be successful.
- You aren't an imposter.
- There isn't a race to success. You get to pick your own pace.
- You need to love yourself.
- "No" doesn't mean to stop asking.

- You are the product of the wonderful people in your life.
- Your emotions are important, but they don't have to rule your life.
- The little things can make the biggest difference.
- You can't fix everything.
- Mondays don't have magic juju that will make your goals easier to achieve.
- When other people win it means more for you, not less.
- You have to be happy now or you'll still be unhappy later.

I'm so glad you've read this far, but I want you to take it one step further. I want you to take my advice and actually act on it. Take something that resonated with you and implement it in your life. Doing different things will create the change you're looking for. You got this book for a reason. Either you or someone you know thought you could benefit from something I said. I hate to tell you, but just reading about my experiences won't make your life better. You can even agree with and memorize all of my good advice. You can read every book I reference in here. None of that will matter until you take the next step and do something about it.

You have a unique set of talents, experiences, and abilities all smooshed into a unique body at this specific time in history. You're one of a kind. This doesn't mean the rules don't apply to you. You're different than I am, but what's true is true regardless of the circumstances. You don't have to believe me, you can do it the hard way, but things will go much smoother if you follow the process.

Unleash the full power of your mind, creativity, love, and weirdness on the world. Don't hold yourself back with lies you've been telling yourself. Permit yourself to be happy, whole, and successful. Remove any roadblock on your success journey, mental or otherwise.

I started with this and I'll end with it:

1. You can have the life you dream about. You deserve it, you're worth it, you can do it.

2. If it's not working, do something about it or change your attitude.

3. You're not alone.

I believe in you. I believe in your dreams, hopes, and desires. I believe that you are capable of more. A.A. Milne is right: "You are braver than you believe, stronger than you seem, and smarter than you think." Friend, you can move mountains. So let's start living those better lives today. Slay those mental monsters and make your dreams come true.

Note From the Author

Thank you for reading my book. In a world filled with (seemingly) endless choices, you chose this book. It is my most heartfelt wish that my stories bring you more than entertainment. I hope that they bring you a step (or a giant leap) closer to living the good life.

I have two favors to ask:

1. **Please leave me a review on Amazon.** Your opinion matters. It can help other people find this book, or it can help me know how to improve in the future.

2. **Stay in touch!** When you create the life you love (or while you're creating it) tell me all about it. I want to know how you overcame the hard things and made something beautiful.
    - www.nikkisoulsby.com
    - Email: author@NikkiSoulsby.com
    - Instagram: @Nikki.Soulsby
    - Facebook: @NikkiSoulsbyAuthor
    - Twitter: @NSoulsby

Notes

1 *The Office*, season 4, episode 14, "Goodbye Toby," directed by Paul Feig, May 15, 2008, NBC.

2 *Pretty Woman*, directed by Garry Marshall, performances by Julia Roberts and Richard Gere (1990: Touchstone Pictures).

3 "Denis Waitley," Goodreads, www.goodreads.com/quotes/26406-it-s-not-what-you-are-that-holds-you-back-it-s.

4 Tony Robbins, Personal Power II, "Day 1," 2006.

5 "A.A. Milne," Goodreads, www.goodreads.com/quotes/6659295-you-are-braver-than-you-believe-stronger-than-you-seem.

6 *The Honeymooners*, performed by Jackie Gleason (1955: CBS).

7 Emily Marsh, "Why We Need to Give More Positive Feedback," T-Three, Jan. 8, 2019, www.t-three.com/soak/insights/why-we-need-to-give-more-positive-feedback.

8 "Change Your Story, Transform Your Life," John Sharp, filmed Nov 2017 at TEDx Beacon Street, Brookline, MA, https://www.ted.com/talks/john_sharp_change_your_story_transform_your_life?language=en.

9 Robin Pogrebin. "Banana Splits: Spoiled by Its Own Success, the $120,000 Fruit Is Gone." *New York Times*, Dec. 8, 2019. https://www.nytimes.com/2019/12/08/arts/design/banana-removed-art-basel.html.

10 Andrew Russeth. "Is Maurizio Cattelan's $120,000 Banana Sculpture a Cynical Sign of the Times or a Thrilling

Artwork? Yes!" *ARTnews.com*, Dec. 8, 2019. www. artnews.com/art-news/news/maurizio-cattelan-banana-basel-1202670910/.

11 Using 2021 prices, a banana is $0.17 and a roll of duct tape from Walmart.com is $3.24. A 6-inch piece of tape to stick a banana to the wall requires about $0.03 worth of tape.

12 Amy Morin. "How Do You Measure Your Self-Worth?" *Psychology Today*, Sussex Publishers, July 11, 2017. www.psychologytoday.com/us/blog/what-mentally-strong-people-dont-do/201707/how-do-you-measure-your-self-worth.

13 "Statistics About Sexual Violence Media Packet," National Sexual Violence Resource Center, www.nsvrc.org/sites/default/files/publications_nsvrc_factsheet_media-packet_statistics-about-sexual-violence_0.pdf.

14 "After Sexual Assault," RAINN, accessed Mar. 8 2021, www.rainn.org/after-sexual-assault.

15 Elyssa Barbash, "Overcoming Sexual Assault: Symptoms & Recovery," *Psychology Today*, Sussex Publishers, Apr. 18, 2017. www.psychologytoday.com/us/blog/trauma-and-hope/201704/overcoming-sexual-assault-symptoms-recovery.

16 Barbash.

17 Marguerite Rigoglioso. "Francis Flynn: If You Want Something, Ask For It." *Stanford Graduate School of Business*, July 1, 2008, www.gsb.stanford.edu/insights/francis-flynn-if-you-want-something-ask-it.

18 David Bach, *The Automatic Millionaire: A Powerful One-Step Plan to Live and Finish Rich*. (Crown Business: 2016).

19 Kimberly Lankford, "6 Ways to Prepare for Medical Expenses in Retirement," *U.S. News & World Report*, Aug. 7, 2020,

money.usnews.com/money/retirement/aging/articles/
preparing-for-medical-expenses-in-retirement.

20 Nerdwallet (https://www.nerdwallet.com/investing/retirement-
    calculator), Dave Ramsey (https://www.daveramsey.com/
    smartvestor/investment-calculator), and Vanguard (https://
    investor.vanguard.com/calculator-tools/retirement-income-
    calculator/).

21 Edward Creagan, "How to Manage Stress and Avoid Overeating
    When Stressed," Mayo Clinic, Aug. 18, 2020, www.
    mayoclinic.org/healthy-lifestyle/stress-management/expert-
    answers/stress/faq-20058497.

22 Jean Antonello, *Naturally Thin: Lasting Weight Loss without
    Dieting* (Heartland Book Company, 2017).

23 Andrew Merle, "This Is When Successful People Wake
    Up," *HuffPost*, July 17, 2017, www.huffpost.com/
    entry/this-is-when-successful-people-wake-
    up_b_596d17a3e4b0376db8b65a1a.

24 Christopher Barnes, "The Ideal Work Schedule, as Determined
    by Circadian Rhythms," *Harvard Business Review*, Jan. 28,
    2015. https://hbr.org/2015/01/the-ideal-work-schedule-as-
    determined-by-circadian-rhythms.

25 https://quotationcelebration.wordpress.com/2017/11/17/a-goal-
    without-a-plan-is-just-a-wish-antoine-de-saint-exupery/

26 Les Brown, "SELF MASTERY - Motivational Speech on
    Success 2017," Dec. 19, 2017, www.youtube.com/
    watch?v=Ypgs3NaJtuE.

27 Roy T. Bennett, *The Light in the Heart* (Roy T. Bennett, 2016).

28 "10 Online Dating Statistics You Should Know (U.S.),"
    eHarmony, 2018, www.eharmony.com/online-dating-
    statistics/.

29 Emily Vogels. "10 Facts about Americans and Online Dating,"
    Pew Research Center, June 4, 2020. www.pewresearch.org/
    fact-tank/2020/02/06/10-facts-about-americans-and-online-
    dating/.

30 Emily Nagoski and Amelia Nagoski. *Burnout: The Secret to
    Unlocking the Stress Cycle.* (New York, NY: Ballantine Books,
    2020).

31 Sebastian Kipman, "15 Highly Successful People Who Failed on
    Their Way to Success," Lifehack, Jan. 21, 2021, www.lifehack.
    org/articles/productivity/15-highly-successful-people-who-
    failed-their-way-success.html.

32 Kipman

33 Kipman

34 R.L. Adams, "21 Famous Failures Who Refused to Give
    Up," *HuffPost*, Sept. 18, 2016, www.huffpost.com/
    entry/21-famous-failures-who-refused-to-give-
    up_b_57da2245e4b04fa361d991ba.

35 Kipman

36 Kipman

37 "J.K Rowling's Wizarding World." *J.K. Rowling*, Feb. 11, 2019,
    https://www.jkrowling.com/writing/.

38 Kipman

39 Adams

40 Adams

41 "Oprah Winfrey." Wikipedia. Accessed June 2, 2018,
    en.wikipedia.org/wiki/oprah_winfrey.

42 Kipman

43 Annie Nova, "10 Highly Successful People on the
    Times They Got Rejected," *Money*, money.

com/10-highly-successful-people-on-the-times-they-got-rejected/.

44   Adams

45   Kfc.com/about

46   Nova

47   Nova

48   Kyle MacDonald, One Red Paperclip. Accesse: 8 Mar. 202. oneredpaperclip.blogspot.com/.

49   Joyce Meyer, "Ask God Boldly! / Daily Devo," Joyce Meyer Ministries, Feb. 20, 2019, joycemeyer.org/dailydevo/2019/02/0220-ask-god-boldly.

50   Jason Ford, "A Self-Made Success? Let's Kill That Myth," *PBS*, Apr. 28, 2017, www.pbs.org/newshour/show/a-self-made-success-lets-kill-that-myth.

51   "5 Main Types of Privilege," Hive Learning, June 12, 2020, www.hivelearning.com/site/5-main-types-of-privileges/.

52   Denise Duffield-Thomas, *Lucky Bitch: A Guide for Exceptional Women to Create Outrageous Success* (New York, NY: Hay House, 2018).

53   Tony Robbins, Personal Power II, "Managing Your State," 2006.

54   Darren Hardy, *The Compound Effect: Multiply Your Success One Simple Step at a Time* (Boston, MA: Da Capo Press, 2013).

55   Jeff Olson and John David Mann, *The Slight Edge: Turning Simple Disciplines into Massive Success and Happiness* (Austin, TX: Greenleaf Book Group, 2013).

56   "Albert Einstein," Goodreads, https://www.goodreads.com/quotes/76863-compound-interest-is-the-eighth-wonder-of-the-world-he.

57   Greg McKeown, *Essentialism: The Disciplined Pursuit of Less* (New York, NY: Crown Publishing Group, 2020).

58   Timothy Ferriss, *The 4-Hour Workweek* (New York, NY: Harmony Books, 2009).

59   Greg McKeown, *Essentialism: The Disciplined Pursuit of Less* (New York, NY: Crown Publishing Group, 2020).

60   "Pareto Principle," Wikipedia. Accessed Jan. 7, 2021, en.wikipedia.org/wiki/Pareto_principle.

61   Gabby Bernstein. "You're Not Responsible for Other People's Happiness," Nov. 18, 2020, gabbybernstein.com/other-peoples-happiness/.

62   Scott Stabile, "Mantra Instagram Inspiration," *Mantra Yoga + Health Magazine*, Jan. 22, 2016, 32.

63   Shankar Vedantam, "How the 'Scarcity Mindset' Can Make Problems Worse," NPR, , Mar. 23, 2017, www.npr.org/2017/03/23/521195903/how-the-scarcity-mindset-can-make-problems-worse.

64   "Four-Minute Mile," Wikipedia. Accessed Feb. 15, 2021. en.wikipedia.org/wiki/Four-minute_mile.

65   Carina Wolff, "Shockingly, These 7 Things Don't Actually Make You Happy, According to Science," *Bustle*, Apr. 12, 2018, www.bustle.com/p/shockingly-these-7-things-dont-actually-make-you-happy-according-to-science-8753299.

66   Wolff

67   *Buckaroo Banzai*, directed by W.D. Richter (1984: Sherwood Productions).

68   https://www.facebook.com/FiveForksAthletics/posts/3587388504642094

69   Linda Alverson-Eiland, et al. "Harnessing Willpower to Meet Your Goals," American Psychological Association, Dec. 9, 2019, www.apa.org/topics/personality/willpower-goals.

70 "Newton's Laws of Motion," Britannica. Accessed March 14, 2021, https://www.britannica.com/science/Newtons-laws-of-motion.

71 "How Long Does It Take for a New Behavior to Become Automatic?" Healthline, Oct. 25, 2019, https://www.healthline.com/health/how-long-does-it-take-to-form-a-habit.

72 "Robert Brault," Goodreads, https://www.goodreads.com/quotes/868414-optimist-someone-who-figures-that-taking-a-step-backward-after.

About the Author

NIKKI SOULSBY is a best-selling author, public speaker, and general badass. A relentless achiever and a lifelong learner, Nikki graduated magna cum laude from Sweet Briar College and received an Executive MBA from Duke University's Fuqua School of Business. She currently works as a leader for a Fortune 50 company and serves on the boards of three national nonprofits. She has been awarded the Triple Crown from Toastmasters International, a green belt in LEAN Six Sigma, and Peak Performance and Skills for Success training from the Dale Carnegie Training.

Nikki's mission is to leave the world better than she found it and help as many people as she can along the way. Using personal experience, research, and proven results, Nikki is teaching people to overcome their limiting beliefs and create their dream life. Her enthusiasm is contagious, her passion is palpable, and her authenticity is refreshing.

She lives in North Carolina with her husband and son. When she's not putting out corporate fires or writing she is reading, ingesting unhealthy amounts of caffeine, or irritating her four cats.

For the latest on writing, rants, and *Lies I Told Myself* visit www.nikkisoulsby.com